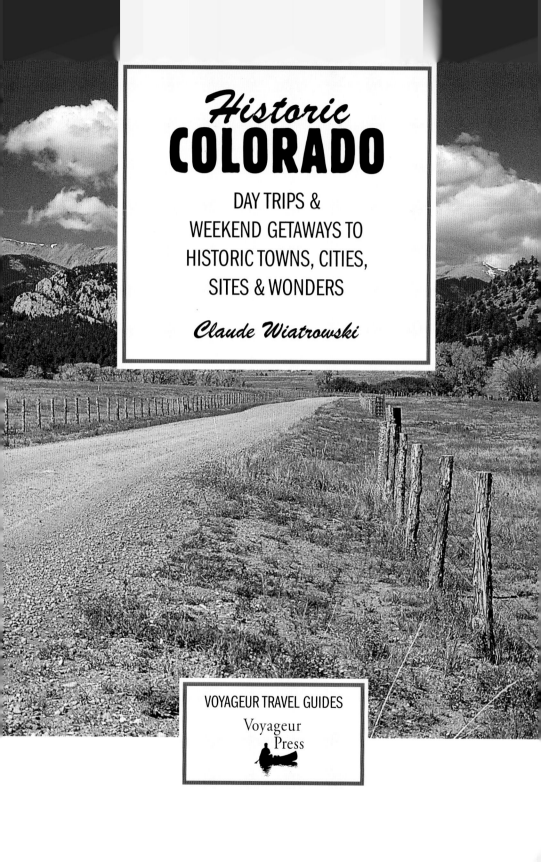

Historic
COLORADO

DAY TRIPS & WEEKEND GETAWAYS TO HISTORIC TOWNS, CITIES, SITES & WONDERS

Claude Wiatrowski

VOYAGEUR TRAVEL GUIDES

Voyageur
Press

First published in 2009 by Voyageur Press, an imprint of MBI Publishing Company, 400 First Avenue North, Suite 300, Minneapolis, MN 55401 USA

Voyageur Press titles are also available at discounts in bulk quantity for industrial or sales-promotional use. For details write to Special Sales Manager at MBI Publishing Company, 400 First Avenue North, Suite 300, Minneapolis, MN 55401 USA.

To find out more about our books, visit us online at www.voyageurpress.com.

ISBN-13: 978-0-7603-3256-6

Library of Congress Cataloging-in-Publication Data
Wiatrowski, Claude A.
  Historic Colorado : day trips & weekend getaways to historic towns, cities, sites & wonders / Claude Wiatrowski.
     p. cm.
  Includes bibliographical references and index.
  ISBN 978-0-7603-3256-6 (softback)
  1. Colorado—History, Local. 2. City and town life—Colorado—History. 3. Colorado—Tours. 4. Cities and towns—Colorado—Guidebooks. 5. Historic sites—Colorado—Guidebooks. 6. Curiosities and wonders—Colorado—Guidebooks. 7. Scenic byways—Colorado—Guidebooks. 8. Automobile travel—Colorado—Guidebooks. I. Title.
  F777.W525 2009
  917.8804'34—dc22
                                        2008042853

Editor: Margret Aldrich
Cover and Text Designer: John Barnett/4 Eyes Design

Printed in China

Title page: There is yet another gorgeous view of the Culebra mountain range as you return from the ghost town of Tercio.

Dedication page: A vintage postcard depicts a glorious view of Pikes Peak.

Contents page: Rim Rock Drive snakes up the canyon at the Fruita entrance to Colorado National Monument.

Dedication

To my wife, Margaret,
whose help and good humor make all my successes possible.

CONTENTS

N144:—BIG THOMPSON CANYON. NEAR ESTES PARK. COLORADO.

41962

Big Thompson Canyon near Estes Park is beautifully depicted in this vintage Colorado postcard.

INTRODUCTION

AMERICAN INDIANS. Conquistadors. Voyageurs. Plainsmen. Mountain men. All dwelled in Colorado. But it was the discovery of gold there in 1858 that began an era of settlement that would overshadow all that had come before. Colorado became a U.S. Territory on February 28, 1861, and the thirty-eighth state—the Centennial State—on August 1, 1876, the year of the one-hundredth anniversary of the country's birth. The first transcontinental railroad, the Union Pacific, had only a modest impact on Colorado, just nicking the northeast corner of the state at Julesburg. But railroads would eventually blanket Colorado's plains as well as its inhospitable mountains, facilitating economic development and enriching its history.

As Americans have become increasingly interested in the history of their country, they have also become interested in exploring the sites where history was made. Heritage tourism is now a major contributor to Colorado's economy. Many isolated historic locations and artifacts were protected by Colorado's rugged mountains, which have preserved ghost towns; mines and mills; railroad tanks, trestles, and tunnels; and more for your enjoyment. With too much from which to choose, I have selected twenty-two journeys, leading you to places that are both historically important and enjoyable to experience. While all of these journeys can be driven in a day, you might want to allocate more time to some if you plan on driving all the optional routings, examining museums in detail, and hiking the trails. In the pages ahead, you'll find location maps, detailed directions to the sites, fascinating information about Colorado's heritage, color photographs of the state's most beautiful and intriguing areas, and vintage images of days gone by.

Not long ago, the greatest threat facing historic artifacts in Colorado was the elements. While isolated locations protected much of Colorado's history from the human destruction that often accompanies development, winter storms slowly ate away at the state's history as artifacts succumbed to the crushing weight of repeated snows. Once considered worthless, the value of these artifacts is now understood, and maintenance has saved many from the harsh elements.

Today, the greatest threat facing Colorado's historic remnants is loss of habitat. Increasingly, cities expand, expensive summer homes are built on old mining claims, large casinos encroach on quaint towns, and energy development scars the landscape. It is impossible to generalize about the wisdom of such development, as each case must be taken individually. In Central City, Blackhawk, and Cripple Creek, for example, it is undeniable that huge, box-like casinos have adversely affected the historic ambiance, but the taxes collected from gambling have been used to fund historic preservation and restoration projects throughout the state. I can tell you that a railroad water tank preserved in a historic railroad yard in a small bucolic town gives the visitor a better sense of its history than does a railroad water tank surrounded by fast-food restaurants and convenience stores in a bustling metropolis. For that reason, this volume emphasizes remote locations over Colorado's largest cities.

Most of the historic places in this book are easy to access on paved roads. A few are on unpaved roads. Since the condition of an unpaved road constantly changes, I recommend that you stop at local visitors' centers, forest service offices, and chambers of commerce for current road information. I would drive any of the unpaved roads mentioned in this book in an ordinary passenger car *that has reasonable ground clearance*, but I normally drive a small SUV and have no trouble getting to any destination listed here. You might disagree. Guidebooks for four-wheel-drive enthusiasts differ on the need for a four-wheel-drive vehicle on some of these roads. Colorado's mountains can be a hostile place, so caution is advised.

Many of Colorado's most interesting historic sites are old mining districts. Visitors should respect fences and "no trespassing" signs—they may be protecting you from

A passenger train crosses the Devil's Gate viaduct on the Georgetown Loop. This 1895 train, traveling downhill toward Georgetown, will soon pass under the famous bridge. *Denver Public Library, Western History Collection, H. S. Poley, P-492*

crashing down a mine shaft that pierces the surface. Except for public tours, never enter a mine, as there may be poisonous gas present or insufficient oxygen to support life.

Needless to say, I can't guarantee that everything included in this book will be exactly as described when you seek it out. Some artifacts may have vanished under the parking lot of a shopping center, while others may have been beautifully restored from the decrepit state shown in this volume.

The maps in this book are simplified and easy to understand. Before setting off on a daytrip, you may want to obtain more detailed maps, especially if you are going far off paved roads. The bibliography lists some sources I use. I also use forest service maps, topographic maps from the U.S. Geological Survey, and maps obtained from specialized sites on the Internet. Many of the backcountry journeys in this book are explained in locally published brochures that include maps with more detailed information about what to see. This is another reason you should stop at visitors' centers and forest service offices where these brochures might be available.

Although this book concentrates on rural Colorado, the larger cities are not ignored. You will want to get detailed street maps of Denver, Colorado Springs, and Pueblo if you wish to explore those cities. You'll find detailed maps useful but not essential for the next largest tier of cities, such as Fort Collins, Loveland, Boulder, and others. Without a street map, you may get lost a few times or have to ask for directions. The less detailed city maps printed on the state map published by the State of Colorado may be all you need, especially for that second tier of cities.

Speaking of getting lost, expect that you'll make a wrong turn once in a while, especially in the most remote places. If a location looks wrong or dangerous, don't proceed. I have listed road numbers as shown on maps, but road numbers are usually not your best guide as you are driving through remote places. Some roads may have multiple numbers: two different county road numbers and a forest road number. Frequently, maps and other reference material use county road and forest road numbers interchangeably. You're more likely to find that the largest, most readable road signs list the *place* you wish to visit and *not* the road number. This is true of the most remote sites described in this book. The directions do not list every historic site mentioned in the main text, so you are advised to read the directions in conjunction with the main text's descriptions.

When I moved to Colorado in 1975, I had more than sixty historical locations on my list of places to visit. After enjoying those and hundreds more, I still have a long list that I'd like to explore. You'll enjoy your travels to the places described in this book and, like me, will find that your historical adventures lead you to even more destinations. Colorado is a treasure house of history, much of it nestled within fantastically beautiful scenery.

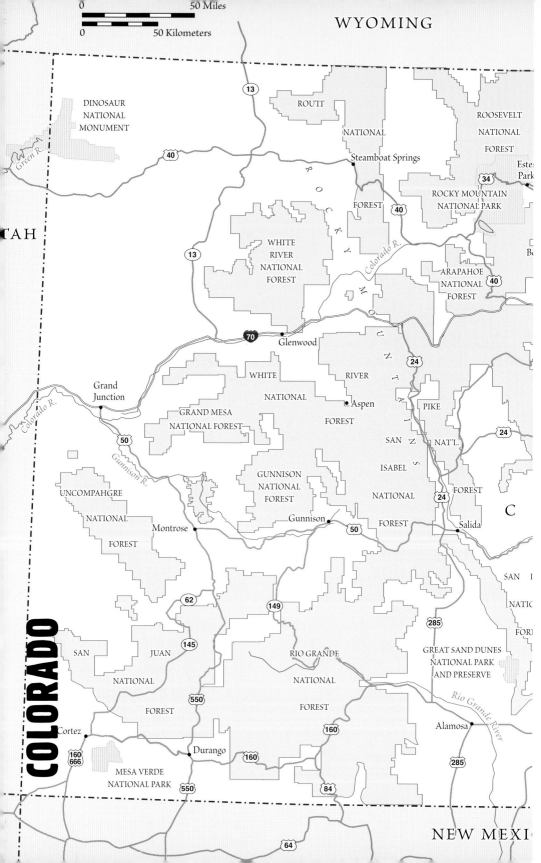

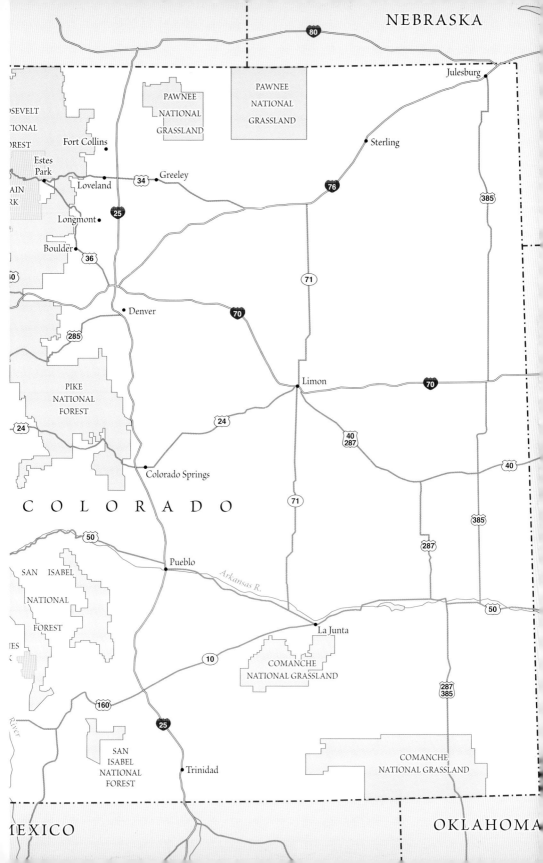

DIRECTIONS

Mack is west of Grand Junction on Interstate 70 at exit 11. From Mack, travel east on I-70 to reach Fruita at exit 19. Take Colorado Highway 340 north and turn right on Aspen Avenue to reach the historic town center. Return to Highway 340, turn left and cross I-70. Turn right on Rim Rock Drive, the entrance to Colorado National Monument. Rim Rock Drive becomes Monument Road as it leaves the monument. Turn right when you reach Highway 340 to continue into Grand Junction. After exploring Grand Junction, follow U.S. Highway 50 southbound and explore Delta's museums and historic downtown. Turn east on Colorado Highway 92 on the north side of Delta. Turn left when you reach Colorado Highway 65 to travel to Orchard City and Cedaredge.

On New Year's Day of 1914, policy changes made parcel post an economical alternative to ordinary railroad freight services for many commodities passing to and from Vernal, Utah, not far from the end of the Uintah Railway's track. Imagine the look on the Salt Lake City postmaster's face when 13,700 bricks, each individually addressed, were mailed to Vernal for construction of a new bank in 1916. The total weight of the bricks came to 35 tons, and the post office routed them via Mack and the Uintah Railway. Parcel-post regulations changed shortly thereafter!

The area around Fruita saw its first settlers in 1882, while the town itself was established two years later. Fruita's citizens could once travel to Grand Junction on an electric interurban railway nicknamed the Fruit Belt Route, a reference to the area's many orchards. Walk around Fruita's well-preserved and attractive historic downtown, a classic town square surrounded by older buildings, northeast of the interstate exit. Dinosaur Journey Museum, located south of this exit, features robotic dinosaurs, dinosaur fossils, and a paleontology laboratory. This is also the route to Colorado National Monument.

Atchee—north of Mack—was host to the shops of the Uintah Railway and was located just south of Baxter Pass, the steepest and most sinuous section of the railroad. *Denver Public Library, Western History Collection, X-6771*

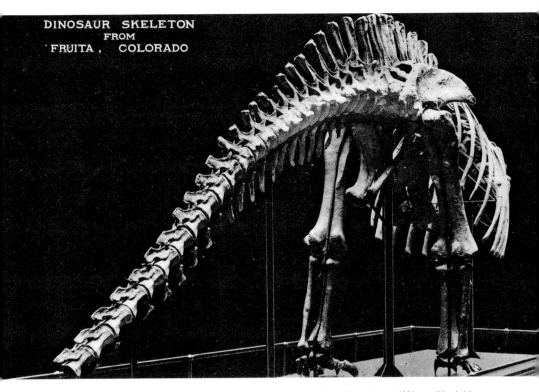

DINOSAUR SKELETON
FROM
FRUITA, COLORADO

The dinosaur skeleton pictured in this vintage postcard was unearthed in Fruita, Colorado, on a 1901 expedition led by Chicago's Field Museum of Natural History.

Colorado National Monument comprises over 20,000 acres of spectacular red rock terrain. In the early nineteenth century, John Otto began exploring this canyon country and constructing trails to make it accessible. It became a national monument on May 24, 1911. Its Rim Rock Drive provides easy access for visitors and is an alternate route to Grand Junction. Hardier souls might consider utilizing the monument's extensive trail system for recreation.

Grand Junction straddles the banks of the Colorado River in an arid valley bounded by the red rock canyons of Colorado National Monument to the southwest, the crenellated spires of the Book Cliffs to the north, and the tree-encrusted, two-mile-high Grand Mesa to the southeast. In 1882, after the resettlement of local Ute Indians in Utah and the construction of the railroad over Marshall Pass (Journey 11), Grand Junction sprang to life. The city's name commemorates the junction of the Grand—now called the Colorado—and Gunnison rivers. From 1882 until the 1960s, Grand Junction's economy was primarily agricultural, as visitors can experience at Cross Orchards Historic Site (3073 F Road). Sugar beets, peaches, pears, and apples left town by the train load. More recently, wineries—many near Palisade—have added grapes to the city's agricultural heritage.

Residents of Grand Junction could light their homes with electricity by 1888 and ride horse-drawn streetcars in 1890. By 1894, they could communicate via telephone. The more studious could attend college classes starting in 1925, and the first building of what would become Mesa State College opened in 1940. It is no surprise that Grand Junction is currently the largest metropolitan area on Colorado's western slope.

Early small-scale coal mining north of town along the Book Cliffs was a harbinger of the importance that energy sources would acquire in the area's economy. More substantial coal resources were developed south of the Grand Mesa in the first half of the twentieth century. In the 1950s, Grand Junction became an important center of the first uranium boom. Oil embargoes of the 1960s created interest in the oil shale deposits northwest of town. Each of these booms sputtered and died as the price of a given energy resource dropped, the cost of extracting that resource rose, or the technology for extraction proved unworkable. Some resources, such as coal, have already regained importance, while new energy sources, including natural gas, have also come into demand. Others are likely to again become prominent in the future.

Grand Junction's beautifully restored downtown includes the 1923 Avalon Theatre (645 Main Street), a venue for the performing arts, as well as the Museum of the West (462 Ute Avenue), one of several sites operated by the Museum of Western Colorado.

Antoine Robidoux established Fort Uncompahgre in 1828 at the confluence of the Uncompahgre and Gunnison rivers as a base for his fur-trading operations. At that time, remote Colorado was home only to mountain men and American Indians, whose paths crossed in 1844 when an Indian attack forced the closing of the fort. The city of Delta grew on the site of the former fort. Like many of Colorado's agricultural centers, Delta has a history heavily influenced by Mormon settlers, though other religious faiths were represented. The Delta County Museum (251 Meeker Street) is a classic pioneer museum with artifacts and exhibits illustrating the area's history as well as an unusual butterfly exhibit. The museum also offers an informative booklet that will guide you to Delta's many substantial historic structures. These include private residences, the Egyptian Theatre (452 Main Street), the First Methodist Episcopal Church

Cross Orchards is one of several museums operated by the Museum of Western Colorado in the Grand Junction area. Outdoor exhibits include portions of the original orchard, which produced mostly apples, and narrow-gauge cars of the Uintah Railway, which once ran trains northeast from Mack.

(now the Delta United Methodist Church at 199 East 5th Street), the Delta Elks Lodge (533 Main Street), and the Municipal Light & Power Plant (1223 Main Street).

Orchard City was incorporated in May of 1912 and would eventually consume the key city of Austin—the railroad shipping point for fruit—as well as two smaller towns, Eckert and Cory. Cedaredge, at the boundary of the Surface Creek valley and the treed Grand Mesa farther north, is home to Pioneer Town (315 SW 3rd Street), a large outdoor museum emphasizing the agricultural history of the region.

Pioneer Town in Cedaredge includes many restored structures as well as some re-creations. Visits begin with a guided tour through many of the museum's buildings.

MARBLE MONUMENT
Marble to Aspen

The Crystal River valley is a remarkable place. The industries of coal mining and marble quarrying and finishing dominated the area in the late nineteenth and early twentieth centuries. Trains of six different railroads chugged or whirred (one was electric) throughout the 40-mile-long valley. There is still much to see along the Crystal River, even near a heavily developed area of Colorado that has lost much of its historic ambiance.

By 1907, teamsters were quarrying blocks of marble southwest of the town of Marble, gingerly transporting them down the mountainside in wagons. Workmen were constructing the marble-finishing mill, some of it built from marble itself! An electric railway, the Yule Tram, began hauling marble from the Yule Marble Quarry in 1910 down a surreally steep track. Eventually, two railroads would haul the huge marble blocks from quarries to the finishing mill. The brilliant white stone was shipped to the rest of the country on the trains of the Crystal River & San Juan Railway.

The marble mill occupied one bank of the Crystal River. In the foreground, you can see trestle pilings—all that remains of the bridge that carried the electric trains of the Yule Tram down from the quarries, loaded with massive marble blocks. The banks of the river are lined with marble to prevent erosion. The large columns functioned as supports for the overhead crane that wrestled the marble blocks about the mill site. A small marble building is visible in the distance in the trees.

Marble for the Lincoln Memorial was wrested from the earth at the Yule Marble Quarry and cut and polished in the mill at Marble. In 1931, the marble block for the Tomb of the Unknown Soldier was quarried here. So heavy was this single block that it was carefully lowered from the quarry to the mill at one mile per day.

Closed in 1917, the mill was rehabilitated and reopened in 1922. The railroad between the mill and quarry was dismantled in 1941. Trucks now carry marble from the quarry down the old, steep railroad grade.

The ruins of the Colorado-Yule Marble Company mill, which extend for about a half mile along the river bank, are fascinating. An operator once stood by the now-rusting conveyor that pokes its head out of a marble-walled building. You can imagine the long-gone overhead crane, struggling with huge blocks of white stone as it rolled along on rails supported by the large marble pillars that still dot the mill site. Farther north, explore the marble graveyard where defective pieces of marble were discarded. (The area is protected, so please do not remove souvenirs.) You can also see marble debris alongside the Crystal River, where it was dumped to stabilize the riverbank. Near the mill parking area in Marble is the turntable pit that spun the locomotives of the Crystal River & San Juan end for end to begin their return journey to Carbondale. That pit was once lined with marble blocks! A small museum in Marble will help you orient yourself to this formerly bustling industrial complex and the town that supported it.

Farther downstream, the white of marble turns to the black of coal at Redstone. A railroad brought coal down from the mines of Coalbasin to be processed into coke at the huge Redstone industrial complex. Coke is mostly carbon, the energy-

DIRECTIONS

Marble is south of Glenwood Springs on County Road 3, just southeast of its junction with Colorado Highway 133. In Marble, turn right on 3rd Street. The ruins of the mill are on the bank of the Crystal River. Drive to the junction with Highway 133 and turn right. As you near Redstone, the Cleveholm mansion will be on your right across the river. Coke oven ruins are farther north on the left, where you will turn right into Redstone to reach the Redstone Inn. Continue north on Highway 133 to reach Carbondale. Just past Carbondale, turn right on Colorado Highway 82. In Basalt, make a left on Midland Avenue to reach the historic downtown.

OPTIONAL: If you want to take the unpaved side trip to the west portals of the Colorado Midland's tunnels, continue east through Basalt on Frying Pan Road (Forest Road 105) to reach Ruedi Reservoir. Continue past the reservoir and turn right on Forest Road 527, which will take you to Lake Ivanhoe and the lower railroad tunnel. You should have detailed maps or local directions, especially if you want to find the upper tunnel.

Return to Highway 82 and turn left toward Aspen. Just before reaching Aspen, you'll encounter a roundabout. Take the Castle Creek Road south to reach Ashcroft. Return to the roundabout, turn right, and continue on Highway 82 into Aspen's historic downtown. Continue east on Highway 82 to visit Independence.

carrying component of coal. The processed coke was shipped to the Colorado Fuel & Iron Company steel mill at Pueblo. Redstone was a company town, with the mining company providing the store, library, town band, and other amenities. Liquor was always a problem in mining towns, but outlawing alcohol never worked; miners simply traveled to the nearest source of the outlawed beverage. John Osgood, the man who developed the Redstone coal complex and fathered the Pueblo steel mill, had a unique solution. The clubs at both Redstone and Coalbasin offered liquor but would not allow one man to buy another a drink. Without the cry of "this round's on me," the endless parade of men reciprocating the favor was averted.

A few remaining coke ovens are adjacent to the highway at Redstone, but they're a tiny fraction of the number that once operated in the formerly huge industrial complex. Not only was coal processed here, but railroad equipment for Redstone's standard- and narrow-gauge railroads was repaired and serviced.

The Redstone Inn building once served as housing for unmarried workers in Redstone's industrial complex. It is now a hotel and restaurant.

A severe depression known as the Silver Panic shut down the railroad to Redstone in 1893, the very year it was constructed, and the trains sat idle until 1899. Coal production ended so suddenly in 1909 that residents had to leave many of their belongings to catch the last train out of Redstone for Carbondale. Osgood attempted to reopen the town's industrial complex many times but without success.

None of Redstone's sizeable industrial plant remains with the exception of some beehive coke ovens near the highway. Drive into town to see the Redstone Inn (82 Redstone Boulevard), now a hotel but originally built in 1901 as housing for single workmen. Osgood built a home here in 1903, a not-so-modest castle named Cleveholm Manor (58 Redstone Boulevard), for a mere $500,000. His castle still stands, though its fortunes have constantly changed. Check to see if tours or lodging might be available. If not, you can glimpse the castle south of town, across the river and through the trees.

Carbondale sits at the north end of the Crystal River, where its waters empty into the Roaring Fork River. Carbondale's roots are agricultural, though its history was strongly influenced by Aspen's silver mines, Redstone's coal mines, and Marble's quarries. The first settlers arrived in the 1880s, and Carbondale was incorporated in 1888. Three railroads—the Crystal River, the Colorado Midland, and the Denver & Rio Grande—once served the town, but none remain. Agriculture has declined in importance, as Carbondale is flanked by two huge tourist destinations: Aspen and Glenwood Springs. Learn about Carbondale's agricultural and coal-mining past at the Mount Sopris Historical Museum (499 Weant Boulevard).

The town of Basalt was once a junction on the spaghetti-like complexity of Colorado's railroad network. Denver & Rio Grande trains from Glenwood Springs whistled through Basalt on their way to Aspen. The Colorado Midland's death-defying crossing of the Continental Divide at Hagerman Pass brought its trains to Basalt, where some continued west to Grand Junction and others branched south to Aspen. The Colorado Midland depot still stands, now a bank in downtown Basalt. The new alignment of Colorado Highway 82 bypasses that road's former path through town, so be sure to jog east through Basalt's old downtown.

You can also drive farther east along an unpaved road, the Colorado Midland Railway grade. There, you'll glimpse the Ruedi Reservoir, drive right by the charcoal ovens at Sellar, traverse the shelf upon which trains perched at Hell Gate

John Osgood's mansion, Cleveholm, still stands at Redstone. It cost $500,000 to build in 1903. The library's walls were covered in green leather hand-tooled with gold. *Denver Public Library, Western History Collection, L. C. McClure, MCC-1969*

(look down and you'll see pieces of a wrecked locomotive tender), and finally enjoy the alpine beauty of Lake Ivanhoe. East of the lake, you can easily spot the lower railroad tunnel, the Busk-Ivanhoe Tunnel. Now called the Carlton Tunnel, it is used to transport water from Colorado's western slope to eastern slope. The higher Hagerman Tunnel is a little more difficult to find, so ask locally or have good maps on hand.

In 1880, optimistic men scurried about to lay claim to five hundred lots at the town site of Ashcroft. By 1881, children skipped along Ashcroft's streets to a public school. Adults waited anxiously for daily mail. Important messages were swiftly conveyed on the electric telegraph wire. By 1885, the town's population peaked at 2,500, though many left during the harsh winters. Along Ashcroft's lively streets, miners stumbled out of seventeen saloons, traveling salesmen struggled with

This was the engineer's view after emerging from the west portal of the Hagerman Tunnel. You can make out the earthen fill in Lake Ivanhoe, which was the railroad's route to the lower Busk-Ivanhoe Tunnel after it was constructed to bypass the higher Hagerman Tunnel through the Continental Divide.

sample cases at eight hotels, and families went bowling. But the sound of the train whistle echoing up the valley from Aspen, just downstream along Castle Creek, was the beginning of the end for Ashcroft. Today it is a ghost town.

In 1953, the town was deeded to the U.S. Forest Service, and in 1974, the Aspen Historical Society began a project to restore and preserve its remaining buildings. There are few Colorado ghost towns with Ashcroft's large stand of old buildings. More importantly, Ashcroft is Colorado's most easily accessed ghost town of its size. It is just 10 miles south of Aspen along a paved road and is handicapped accessible. If you want to experience an authentic Colorado ghost town without an adventurous road trip, Ashcroft is your destination.

In 1879, prospectors discovered silver in the Roaring Fork valley, nestled between the Sawatch Range and Elk Mountains; Aspen was incorporated just a year later. Mines bustled with activity, and a smelter gushed noxious fumes into the sky, creating wealth in the process. All that was missing to ensure prosperity was reliable and efficient transportation. After two railroads, the Colorado Midland and the Denver & Rio Grande, arrived in 1887, Aspen boomed. The 1890 Sherman Silver Purchase Act, which required the federal government to purchase 4.5 million ounces of silver monthly, increased Aspen's fortunes. It was Colorado's third largest city by 1892, with over twelve thousand residents. Trolleys, churches, saloons, prostitution, gambling—Aspen had everything a wealthy mining town needed! The repeal of the Sherman Silver Purchase Act in 1893, however, devastated Aspen as it did all of Colorado's silvered cities.

Aspen's miners hiked up the slopes above town to reach work and slid down on "boards" to return home. The region's first ski resort, at Ashcroft, appeared in the 1930s, but it was not until after World War II that Aspen's now famous ski industry blossomed. Also after the war, summer cultural activities began to grow in Aspen with the support of Chicago industrialist Walter Paepcke. Music festivals, scientific conferences, and instructional programs continue to fill the summer months.

Aspen's downtown is home to many restored historic structures, including the Wheeler Opera House (320 E Hyman Avenue) and the Hotel Jerome (330 E Main Street). The Wheeler/Stallard Museum (620 W Bleeker Street) chronicles Aspen's history; it is one of several facilities operated by the Aspen Historical Society. East of Aspen, the ghost town of Independence is adjacent to the Independence Pass road, which is closed each winter by mounds of snow.

The Hotel View in Ashcroft was aptly named. One of many buildings maintained by the Aspen Historical Society, it actually collapsed in 1974 and was re-erected by the Historical Society and the U.S. Forest Service. It was once a hotel, a brothel, and a Chinese restaurant!

A miner appears to be taking his children on a ride to work in 1890. Aspen's magnificent commercial district is visible in the distance. *Library of Congress, Kilburn Brothers, LC-USZ62-117984*

DINOSAUR RANCH
Northwest of New Castle

New Castle was incorporated in 1888 in response to newly discovered coal deposits. As luck would have it, the mines were exceptional sources of explosive methane gas. After several fires and explosions between 1896 and 1918, the last mine closed permanently. Making lemonade from lemons, New Castle hosts the annual Burning Mountain Festival, named after nearby coal mines that are still ablaze underground. The town features historic buildings and the New Castle Historical Museum (in the original 1893 town hall and fire station at 116 North 4th Street).

Rifle began to take shape in 1882 but was not incorporated until 1905. Lights flickered to life in Rifle in 1910 as one of Colorado's first hydroelectric plants whirred into operation. A ranching town, Rifle was the most important stock shipping point in Colorado where livestock were loaded onto railroad cars. Farming also played a part in the city's economy. In the last half of the twentieth century, mining of vanadium, uranium, coal, and oil shale were added to the mix. The Rifle Creek Museum (337 East Avenue) is located in the former city hall.

Rifle Falls State Park, north of the town of Rifle, is near the site of one of the earliest hydroelectric plants in Colorado.

DIRECTIONS

N
W   E
S

New Castle is just west of Glenwood Springs at Interstate 70, exit 105. Follow U.S. Highway 6 west from New Castle through Silt to Rifle. At Rifle, turn right on Colorado Highway 13 to reach Meeker. After exploring Meeker, double back on Highway 13 to its junction with Colorado Highway 64, which you should follow northwest to Rangely. Continue on Highway 64 until it ends and turn left on U.S. Highway 40. Turn right on Utah Highway 149 to reach the entrance to Dinosaur National Monument. The Josie Bassett Morris Cabin is on Cub Creek Road. Return to U.S. 40 and turn left to reach the Colorado entrance to the monument. At that entrance, follow Harpers Corner Road north into the monument's scenic canyon country.

Nathanial Meeker was appointed Indian agent for the White River Ute Indian Reservation in 1878. He had come to Colorado in 1870 to found the Union Colony, a utopian religious community, near Greeley (Journey 6). Meeker regarded the Utes as savages and was determined to "reform" them into God-fearing farmers. The Utes rebelled on September 29, 1879, killing Meeker and other male agency employees and taking women and children hostage. The U.S. Army soon arrived to quell the rebellion. Their officers' quarters, built in 1880, now house the White River Museum (565 Park Avenue) in the town of Meeker, which was founded in 1883 after the army left. In 1887, settlers attacked nearby Utes without provocation, and eventually, the Colorado militia joined the fray. Some historians consider this the last major altercation between U.S. settlers and Native Americans in the Old West.

Rangely was founded in 1880 as a trading post but not incorporated until the late date of 1947. The Rangely Outdoor Museum (150 Kennedy Drive) chronicles the varied history of the region. Ranching and farming were followed by the development of oil fields, coal mines, and gilsonite mines. The area is rich in Native American history, and there are many rock art sites nearby.

Although the great Colorado dinosaur rush began in 1877 near Morrison (Journey 8), discoveries were made throughout Colorado. In 1909, an enormous

Meeker's St. James Parish dates from 1888, just one year after the last major confrontation between settlers and Ute Indians occurred north of Meeker. It was one of the first Episcopal churches in Colorado.

Just visible on the other side of Steamboat Rock, the Yampa River (background) flows into the Green River (foreground) at Echo Park in Dinosaur National Monument.

deposit of fossil dinosaur bones was uncovered in northeastern Utah by Earl Douglass. Douglass excavated there for fifteen years, shipping over 350 tons of fossils to the Carnegie Museum in Pittsburgh, Pennsylvania. His quarry site became Dinosaur National Monument in 1915; the monument was greatly expanded in 1938 to include a large area of Colorado. Its 200,000 acres encompass the junction of the Yampa and Green rivers.

Imagine the courage required for Josie Bassett Morris, a single woman, to homestead a ranch in 1914 in the remoteness of what is now Dinosaur National Monument. Imagine her living here for fifty years without running water, telephone, or electricity. Her cabin is preserved in its original isolated and beautiful location on Cub Creek. Other historic ranches are also located within the monument, but the Morris homestead is easily reached by automobile.

You can reach the Josie Morris Cabin along Cub Creek from the Utah portion of Dinosaur National Monument. Morris ranched here by herself for fifty years.

MOFFAT COUNTRY
Craig to Glenwood Springs

Craig was founded in 1889. The Moffat railroad chugged to a halt here and provided an avenue for economic development. Though Craig's first decades were dominated by ranching and agriculture, it has long been a city of energy. Nearby coal deposits first attracted the railroad's steel rails like a magnet. Oil, natural gas, and even uranium added to the city's reputation as a center of energy development. Craig's Museum of Northwest Colorado (590 Yampa Avenue) reflects the city's varied background and includes informative exhibits on topics from coal mining and farming to gunfighters and the Moffat railroad. The most impressive historical artifact in Craig is David Moffat's private railroad car, Marcia, named for his daughter. The car is located in City Park at Washington Street and westbound U.S. Highway 40 (Victory Way).

DIRECTIONS

From Craig, travel east on U.S. Highway 40 to Steamboat Springs. Continue on U.S. 40 eastbound and turn right on Colorado Highway 131. Travel though Oak Creek, Phippsburg, Yampa, and Bond to join Interstate 70 near Wolcott. Travel west on I-70 through Glenwood Canyon to Glenwood Springs. The historic area of Glenwood Springs is best reached from exit 116. Follow the signs for Grand Avenue and Colorado Highway 82.

Steamboat Springs owes its unusual name to the raucous blast made by one of its natural mineral springs, a sound mistaken for a steamboat by French trappers in the early nineteenth century. There are more than 150 springs in the area. Raising livestock was big business here, especially after the railroad's arrival provided a vital transportation artery to the rest of the country. Coal eventually surpassed cattle, also because of the railroad, though agriculture is still important in the region.

DAVID MOFFAT AND HIS RAILROAD

DAVID MOFFAT ARRIVED in Denver in 1860 seeking his fortune. Over the next four decades, he became a banker and Colorado's wealthiest citizen. Moffat personally financed a solution to Denver's transportation conundrum by constructing the Denver, Northwestern & Pacific Railway, which was begun in 1902. Both the Union Pacific and the Denver & Rio Grande saw the Moffat (its long-term nickname) as a competitor and obstructed its progress. They needn't have bothered, for the mountainous terrain proved to be a sufficient obstruction.

The Moffat looked to northwestern Colorado coal to sustain it while its construction extended to the Pacific Ocean. Trains reached Craig in 1911, but the inability to raise capital at the end of America's railroad-building frenzy meant that the mainline would never get closer to the great western ocean. The railroad hauled coal over 11,660-foot Rollins Pass (Journey 7) with corkscrew track and snow higher than an elephant's eye. An extra ton of coal lugged over this monster pass actually *reduced* the railroad's profits. A tunnel under Rollins Pass was the only solution, and Moffat secured financing to build that tunnel in 1911. Union Pacific spies overheard Moffat mention this success, and they pressured investors to withdraw. Moffat died the next day. Some say he committed suicide, but the cause of his death has never been confirmed. Without Moffat at the helm, there would be no new investors, and the railroad went bankrupt within months. Reorganized as the Denver & Salt Lake, it would never even reach Salt Lake City.

Years later, a publicly financed tunnel was driven under Rollins Pass. With the completion of the Dotsero Cutoff (Journey 4), which connected the two former enemies, Denver & Rio Grande trains detoured over the Moffat and saved 175 miles on their way to Salt Lake City. The Moffat was merged into the Rio Grande in 1947.

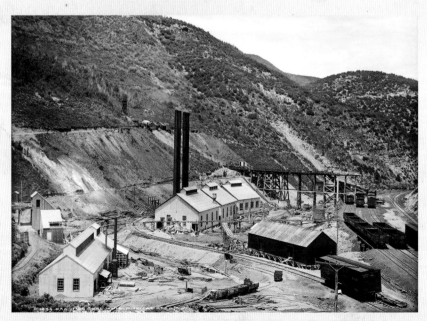

The Oak Creek Coal Mine was one of many served by Moffat's railroad. *Denver Public Library, Western History Collection, L. C. McClure, MCC-1099*

Children prepare to race on the snow-covered street of Steamboat Springs in this undated photograph taken sometime after World War I. *Denver Public Library, Western History Collection, L. C. McClure, MCC-2434*

As in much of Colorado's mountainous territory, skiing was vital to pioneer residents of Steamboat Springs—not as recreation but because it provided the only viable means of locomotion during the winter's snows. A new sort of pioneer, Carl Howelsen, arrived in Steamboat Springs in 1913 with the odd notion that skiing could be fun. Howelsen organized Steamboat's first winter carnival as a vehicle to introduce competitive skiing and as a celebration of the season—a novel idea in 1914! A major ski area now covers the slopes of Mount Werner just east of town.

Browse the Tread of Pioneers Museum (800 Oak Street), which includes a history of skiing in the Steamboat Springs area. Coal trains still rumble by the Moffat railroad's depot, preserved as the Eleanor Bliss Center for the Arts at the Depot (1001 13th Street).

Small coal mines began hauling coal by wagon as early as 1887. However, it took the arrival of the Moffat railroad to make coal a big business, and it took the big business of coal to keep the struggling trains in operation. Arriving in 1909, the railroad's influence on Oak Creek is typical of a railroad's arrival everywhere in Colorado. A lumberyard, a dairy, a laundry, a drugstore, barbershops, two saloons, and a Methodist-Episcopal Church all opened here that same year. Enjoy the small but interesting roadside exhibit in downtown Oak Creek, which interprets the area's coal-mining history.

A small but informative roadside exhibit at Oak Creek explains the Yampa Valley's coal-mining history.

As a result of inhumane working conditions, a 1913 coal miners' strike in southern Colorado soon spread to Oak Creek. By Christmas, a riot had ensued, and violence became the norm. Coal production from underground mines dwindled with the Great Depression and essentially ended with World War II. After the war, strip mining began. Coal remains a major industry in the area.

The town of Phippsburg was large enough to merit the opening of a post office in 1884. Phippsburg became an important railroad center when the Moffat line chose to make it a division point where locomotives were serviced and crews changed. It is still a significant railroad town.

Before the Moffat railroad arrived, supplies were hauled into the area by wagon from the nearest Denver & Rio Grande track at Wolcott. Yampa, called Egeria until 1886, was the gateway for those supplies. A dozen sawmills operated here to meet Routt County's need for lumber. Pull off the highway onto Moffat Avenue, an incredibly wide boulevard once needed to handle the commercial traffic in this now sleepy town.

It never hurt a small town's economy to name its main street after a railroad president, as was the case with Moffat Avenue in Yampa. The wide boulevard was necessary during the period when substantial commerce passed through Yampa.

The Dotsero Cutoff was a railroad track built to connect two railroads, the Moffat at Bond and the Denver & Rio Grande at Dotsero. Its 1934 opening provided such an important shortcut between Denver and Salt Lake City that the miraculous new diesel-powered streamlined train, the Burlington *Zephyr*, traveled to the remote junction of Bond to celebrate.

In 1860, Captain Richard Sopris was the first European to relax in the hot springs that are the centerpiece of Glenwood Springs. Health-seeking tourists easily reached the sizzling pools in 1887 after the Denver & Rio Grande—the first of two railroads—arrived via a railroad grade blasted into the south wall of Glenwood Canyon. John Henry "Doc" Holliday, the dentist turned legendary gunfighter, came to Glenwood Springs on the new railroad that year along with his longtime friend Wyatt Earp. Just a few months later, Doc died of the tuberculosis that had plagued him most of his life, instead of violently passing in a shootout as he had expected. Doc Holliday is buried at Linwood Pioneer Cemetery (trailhead at 12th Street and Bennett Avenue).

By 1890, development included a stone bathhouse next to the hot-springs pool, and it was clear that Glenwood Springs was destined to be popular with tourists. Now as then, there is much to see. Visit the historic train depot (413 7th Street), now the Glenwood Railroad Museum as well as a stop for Amtrak passenger trains. Enjoy the 1893 Hotel Colorado (526 Pine Street), more elegant than ever after a post–World War II restoration. Theodore Roosevelt relaxed at the Hotel Colorado, and when its maids presented him with a small stuffed bear, his daughter christened it a Teddy Bear—a name still with us today. Stop at the Frontier Historical Museum (1001 Colorado Avenue) and walk around the historic downtown. First opened to the public in 1895, the Fairy Caves were closed in 1917, then reopened in 1999 as part of the Glenwood Caverns Adventure Park (51000 Two Rivers Plaza Road). And of course, you can still relax in the hot springs.

When I moved to Colorado in 1975, Interstate 70 dissolved into a minor two-lane road on the north side of the river east of Glenwood Springs, probably the last gap in the originally conceived Interstate Highway System. The gap remained for many years because the construction of a conventional multilane highway through the canyon would have destroyed much of its beauty. As a result of continued public pressure, the Interstate Highway System's most environmentally sensitive segment was eventually built here, completed in 1992 after a dozen years of construction.

The Rio Grande *Zephyr* snakes its way through Glenwood Canyon on the south bank of the Colorado River. These were the rails that first reached Glenwood Springs and spurred its development.

The roof in the foreground is the Glenwood Springs Depot, while the building beyond—actually across the Colorado River—is the bathhouse for the hot springs. The lofty structure even farther distant is the Hotel Colorado.

THE NORTHEAST
Gold & Grain

NORTHEASTERN COLORADO'S diverse history was shaped by Native Americans, farmers, miners, and eventually tourists. This beautiful region was home to plains Indians long before European or U.S. settlers arrived. Those settlers traveled to Colorado in wagon trains on the Overland Trail, an alternate route that bypassed a portion of the Oregon Trail subject to Indian attacks. They came to farm on Colorado's eastern plains and established a cooperative agricultural colony at Greeley by 1870. One year earlier, the fledgling transcontinental railroad touched the northeast corner of the state, and a white settlement boom followed. Colorado's first gold rush—called the Pikes Peak Gold Rush, though it was not near Pikes Peak—ushered in the era of mountain railroading as narrow-gauge trains wobbled up Clear Creek to the mines. The region's first tourists traveled into the mountains in comfort on that same little railroad, and subsequent visitors began a long tradition of enjoying the spectacular scenery in Rocky Mountain National Park.

One-hundred-fifty lakes and 450 miles of streams decorate Rocky Mountain National Park.

0   50 Miles

0   50 Kilometers

ROOSEVELT NATIONAL FOREST

25

85

14

Laporte

Fort Collins

14   Ault

ROCKY MOUNTAIN

34   Estes Park

Loveland

34   Greeley

Big Thompson R.

ROUTT NATIONAL FOREST

NATIONAL PARK

36

Grand Lake

7

Lyons

287

66   Longmont   Platteville

40

9

5

7

Byers Canyon

Kremmling

Granby

40

Hot Sulphur Springs

72

36

6

119   Boulder

40

Rollins Pass

149   Rollinsville

36

85

ARAPAHOE NATIONAL FOREST

Winter Park

7

Central City Pkwy.

GORE RANGE

9

Central City

Golden

70

6

Silverthorne

Georgetown

70

Georgetown Loop RR

74   Morrison

•Denver

Frisco

▲ Mt. Evans

South Platte R.

ROCKY MOUNTAINS

Boreas Pass Rd.

Breckenridge

285

24

Boreas Pass

8

Pine   South Platte

91

9

33

Bailey

South Platte River Road

Alma

Como

126

Leadville

Fairplay

PIKE

67

PIKE

NATIONAL

82

285

9

FOREST

Arkansas R.

24

Woodland Park

NAT'L.

Trout Creek Pass

SAN

ISABEL

NATIONAL

24

FOREST

Colorado Springs

115

Salida

50

Arkansas R.

50

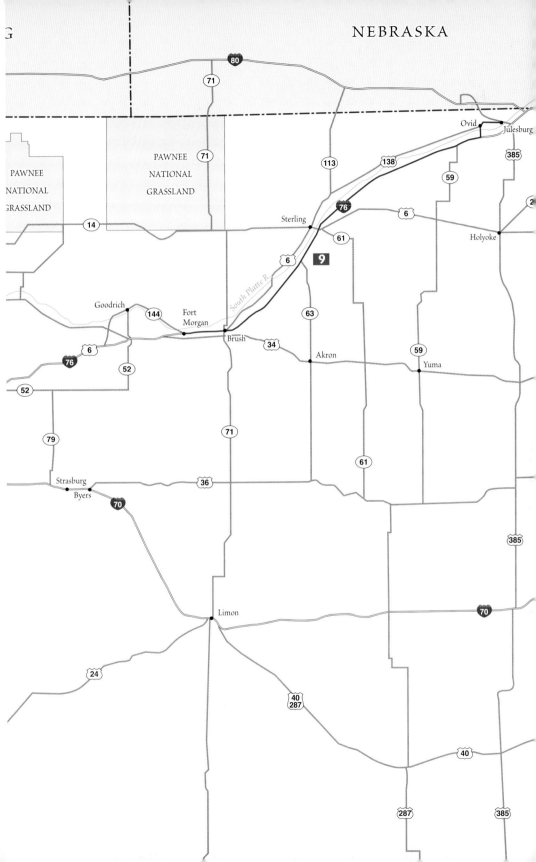

GREAT GATEWAY
Across Rocky Mountain National Park

This journey will take you across Colorado's Middle Park. In Colorado, park describes a flat-bottomed, high-altitude mountain valley. Colorado has three large parks: North Park, Middle Park, and South Park. Some would also include the San Luis Valley and the Gunnison Valley in the list of Colorado's largest parks. Parks do not have to be huge: Silverton nestles in southwestern Colorado's tiny Bakers Park (Journey 15).

In 1884, Rudolph Kremmling established a general store on the north bank of Muddy Creek at the location of the town that one day would be named after him. By 1904, a small ranching community had developed there, with 140 hardy souls braving the harsh Middle Park winters. These pioneers celebrated the arrival of the Moffat railroad in 1906, ending their chilly isolation.

Farther east, Ute Indians as well as white hunters and trappers all settled near the therapeutic, hot bubbling pools of the region, peacefully coexisting while they healed their pains in the magic elixir. By 1864, this place was called Hot Sulphur Springs. The railroad's arrival attracted tourists to the healing springs, and they are still a popular spa destination today. Many historic structures can be seen in Hot Sulphur Springs, but don't miss the Grand County Historical Association's

DIRECTIONS

Kremmling is at the junction of Colorado Highway 9 and U.S. Highway 40. Travel east on U.S. 40 through Hot Sulphur Springs. Turn left on U.S. Highway 34 to reach Grand Lake; then pass through Rocky Mountain National Park to Estes Park. U.S. 34 is closed through Rocky Mountain National Park in the winter. Continue east on U.S. 34 to reach Loveland and the end of your journey.

Pioneer Village (110 East Byers Avenue), which features an old school building that houses the best interpretive museum in Colorado. Don't be fooled by the building's unimpressive exterior; be sure to enter and spend time in the exhibits. Subject after subject—every Grand County town, pioneers, winter sports, a World War II POW camp, pioneer women, the Moffat railroad—is explained through words, photos, and artifacts. You can make a quick pass, reading just a little at each exhibit, or take a leisurely stroll, reading every word and studying every image. Learn about Grand County in as much or as little time as you want to spend.

This panoramic photo of Hot Sulphur Springs was created in 1910 with the photographer's lens pointed southeast. The Moffat railroad yards are in the foreground; the town lies across the Colorado River. The steam-powered freight train at right will soon dive into Byers Canyon. *Library of Congress, E. F. Sawdey & R. B. Hindmarsh, PAN US HEOG-Colorado No. 28*

Granby was founded in 1905, coinciding with the arrival of the Moffat railroad and established for the railroad's convenience. In 1907, the Rocky Mountain Railroad began construction of its short track at a connection with the Moffat at Granby. That track continued up the Grand River to lumber mills and logging camps. Its rails lasted a scant ten years. Granby became a commercial center and the gateway to Grand Lake, itself the gateway to Rocky Mountain National Park.

The Grand County Courthouse and Jail is one of the historic structures in the Grand County Historical Association's Pioneer Village in Hot Sulphur Springs, but the site's indoor exhibits—some of the finest in Colorado—are the best reason to visit.

Grand Lake—at the western entrance to Rocky Mountain National Park—is much smaller than Estes Park, which lies at the park's eastern entrance. Grand Lake retains more of the atmosphere of frontier tourism, with some residences standing since the nineteenth century. The Kauffman House Museum (407 Pitkin), Grand Lake's last log hotel structure, combines local history with a spectacular view of the lake itself.

The Kauffman House was a hotel as well as a residence. It is the last surviving log hotel—now a museum—representative of Grand Lake during the early days of tourism in Rocky Mountain National Park and has a spectacular view of the lake.

"DOC SUSIE" ANDERSON

BORN IN FORT WAYNE, INDIANA, Susan Anderson graduated from the University of Michigan medical school in 1897. She moved to Cripple Creek, Colorado, where her family lived, to set up a practice but later made her way to Denver. Eventually, she ended up in Greeley working as a nurse, as acceptance of women doctors was far from universal.

When Anderson's mild case of tuberculosis worsened, she moved to Middle Park because a cold and dry climate was thought to have curative properties. Initially incognito, she was soon discovered to be the fine doctor she was and began a long and distinguished career as a physician. As Grand County coroner during the construction of the Moffat Tunnel, Doc Susie fought the Tunnel Commission for safer working conditions. By one estimate, the tunnel cost nineteen lives in addition to hundreds injured. Anderson continued to heal the sick and injured until 1956; she died in 1960.

A young Susan Anderson stands at the door to her cabin in Cripple Creek. *Denver Public Library, Western History Collection, Andrew James Harlan, Z-141*

Ute Indians once hunted in the high mountains that became Rocky Mountain National Park. Major Stephen H. Long, a U.S. military officer, explorer, and engineer, led the first scientific expedition on the Platte River in 1820. On that expedition, Long caught sight of the peak that would later bear his name and would become a centerpiece of the park, but he avoided it and the hostile territory nearby.

As early as 1867, the region became a destination for visitors and not just explorers. In 1860, Kentuckian Joel Estes spotted the valley in which the town

Most of Colorado's roads attempt to avoid the highest mountains, but the main road through Rocky Mountain National Park deliberately scurries atop them for many miles. Called Trail Ridge Road, this 12,183-foot-high wonder is also U.S. Highway 34. Its highest portion is closed in winter.

of Estes Park would come to be. Seven years later, Estes gave up ranching and opened guest accommodations for visitors to the scenic area. Mining, farming, and ranching were all attempted in the region without success. In the end, Estes Park would rely on its greatest natural resource: the natural beauty of the mountains and all they contained.

F. O. Stanley arrived in Estes Park in 1903 and helped establish the Estes Park Protective and Improvement Association to safeguard the area's natural beauty. Enos Mills, who arrived in 1884 at the age of fourteen, proposed during the early twentieth century that the area around Longs Peak become a national park. Rocky Mountain National Park was created in January 1915. The park encompasses 415 square miles of rugged, spectacular scenery. Enos Mills Cabin (6760 Colorado Highway 7) is a small museum south of Estes Park.

F. O. Stanley built the grand Stanley Hotel (333 Wonderview Avenue) in 1909, and it is still a popular destination. This is the hotel that inspired Stephen King's novel *The Shining*. Stanley constructed the road from Lyons to Estes Park, and Stanley Steamer automobiles transported guests to his hotel from the Burlington Railroad depot at Lyons. In a day when everyone traveled long distances by train, this novelty predicted the eventual shift from trains to autos. Stanley also built the Fall River Hydro Plant (1754 Fish Hatchery Road) to

N125:—THE STANLEY HOTEL AT ESTES PARK. COLORADO.

The Stanley Hotel—pictured here in a vintage postcard—has been a favorite resort for thousands of Colorado visitors.

power his hotel in this isolated wilderness. Continuing to generate electricity until it was damaged by a flood in 1982, the plant is now a museum. The Estes Park Museum (200 4th Street) interprets local history, and the Lula W. Dorsey Museum (2515 Tunnel Road), located at the YMCA of the Rockies, chronicles that camp's history. Tourists can also visit an 1896 homestead at the MacGregor Ranch Museum (180 MacGregor Lane).

Loveland originated, quite literally, from a field of wheat. When David Barnes heard that the Colorado Central Railroad was going to lay a track from Denver to Cheyenne through his wheat field, he had the foresight to plat a town site and name it Loveland in honor of the railroad's president! Not surprisingly, the town prospered. Nearby localities were abandoned as their population moved closer to the railroad, which constructed its first Loveland depot in late 1877. The town's first commercial business, a two-story brick dry-goods store, opened at the beginning of 1878, just a month after the depot was completed. Today's Loveland Museum/Gallery (503 North Lincoln Avenue) includes local history exhibits, one of which describes a unique service: Starting in the 1940s, volunteers began remailing Valentine's Day cards sent to "The Sweetheart City" so that they would carry its special postmark. The program continues today. In a two-week period every year, tens of thousands of affectionate cards and letters leave Loveland, stamped by volunteers with a romantic illustration and poem.

GO WEST, YOUNG MAN
The Northern Front Range

Camp Collins came into being in 1862 at what is now Laporte to protect the Overland Mail Route from Indian attack. The camp was wiped out by a flood that surged down the Cache la Poudre River in 1864, and Fort Collins was erected nearby. The fort was decommissioned in 1867, but by then civilian settlers had begun to arrive. The town was incorporated in 1873, shortly after the U.S. government opened the land for settlement. Fort Collins' first railroad, the Colorado Central, arrived in 1877 to set the stage for economic growth. Substantial commercial and residential structures began to rise from the prairie, including an opera house, that seemingly universal symbol of prosperity and culture in the American West. Colorado Agricultural College, now Colorado State University, opened its doors in 1879. Fort Collins' citizens knew by then that their home would become more than a minor agricultural community.

DIRECTIONS

Travel east from Fort Collins on Colorado Highway 14. Turn right on U.S. Highway 85 to reach Greeley. In Greeley, take Business Route 85 (8th Avenue) and turn west on A Street to reach Centennial Village. Continue south on Route 85 to reach Platteville. The Fort Vasquez Museum is just south of Platteville on U.S. 85. Return to Platteville and head west on Colorado Highway 66. Turn left on U.S. Highway 287 to see Longmont; then return to U.S. 66. Turn left to reach Lyons. Explore Lyons and return east on Highway 287 to turn right on U.S. Highway 36, which will lead you to Boulder.

From 1907 until 1951, residents of Fort Collins rode the streetcar system to work, to church, to the park, to shops, even to the cemetery. A small portion of the streetcar system was restored in 1984, and visitors can ride an original Fort Collins streetcar down Mountain Avenue. Don't miss Old Town with its copious supply of lovely old commercial structures. The Old Town area is anchored

A restored Fort Collins Municipal Railway trolley car waits for riders on Mountain Avenue at the St. Joseph Church. The tiny four-wheeled trolleys—many cities used eight-wheeled cars—were the mainstay of the Fort Collins system, and several still exist.

by Old Town Square at the corner of North College and Mountain avenues. Other historic sites include the Avery House (328 W Mountain Avenue), Fort Collins Waterworks (2005 North Overland Trail), the Romero House (425 10th Street)—now the Museo de las Tres Colonias—and the Fort Collins Museum (200 Mathews Street).

Fort Latham, a stagecoach stop on the Overland Trail, was constructed in 1864 at the junction of the South Platte and Cache la Poudre rivers. Nathanial Meeker founded the Union Colony—a cooperative agricultural venture—here in 1870 before his ill-fated appointment to the White River Ute Indian Reservation (Journey 3). The Union Colony was renamed Greeley in honor of Horace Greeley, who had been Meeker's editor at the *New York Tribune*. Greeley, who advocated settlement of the American West, is best known for his advice to "Go west, young man." Enjoy a pleasant and informative walk though forty-five restored historic structures at Greeley's Centennial Village Museum (1475 A Street). Visit the Greeley History Museum (714 8th Street) in the huge, 34,000-square-foot historic *Greeley Tribune* building. Meeker's home is now the Meeker Museum (1324 9th Avenue).

The Stevens House was moved to Greeley's Centennial Village in 1975. It is an eleven-room residence built in the Queen Anne style in 1900.

Evans, established in 1867, is adjacent to and south of Greeley and houses the Evans Historical Museum (3720 Golden Street) in a restored Victorian residence. Evans was originally a railroad town on the Denver Pacific Railroad, which provided Denver with a critical connection to the Union Pacific transcontinental railroad at Cheyenne. As its importance as a railroad center declined, Evans centered itself around agriculture.

Mountain men trapped animals, primarily beaver, and sold their furs at an annual rendezvous for use as fashionable hats. Sometimes pelts were obtained by trading with Indians as well. It was a rough way to make a living in remote Colorado in the early nineteenth century. Louis Vasquez and Andrew Sublette established a fur-trading enterprise in 1835—just as silk was replacing beaver in hat construction—near what would become Platteville. In 1932, the Fort Vasquez Museum (13412 U.S. Highway 85) was reconstructed on its ruins. The museum chronicles Colorado's economic history during these decades of westward expansion.

Longmont was founded in 1871 as the Chicago-Colorado Colony and became a major player in the agricultural richness of the northern Front Range after the Colorado Central Railroad arrived in 1877. The Longmont Museum (400 Quail

At Centennial Village, this 1885 pavilion at Hanna Square anchors the Central Village area and is surrounded by structures representative of Greeley's diverse population between 1870 and 1920. You'll explore a railroad depot, church, school, and several residences.

Road) was established in 1936 by the St. Vrain Historical Society. Now operated by the City of Longmont, it shares a building with the city's cultural center. Here, in a modern setting, you can find exhibits about the history of both Longmont and the St. Vrain River Valley.

Edward Lyon saw the economic potential of the hard red sandstone he had discovered near present-day Lyons and quarried and sold that material for constructing buildings. Business improved after 1885, when the trains of the Denver, Utah & Pacific offered an economical way to transport the attractive material. The University of Colorado's new sandstone campus, constructed before World War I, marked the end of major quarrying activities near Lyons as other materials replaced sandstone. The Denver, Utah & Pacific would later become part of the Burlington Railroad and would make Lyons an important gateway to Rocky Mountain National Park (Journey 5). Explore the sandstone structures in the Lyons Historic District and stop at the Lyons Redstone Museum (338 High Street).

Prospectors found gold in the mountains west of present-day Boulder in 1858. The mining of gold, silver, and coal was a prominent part of Boulder's economy for a century. The Boulder City Town Company was organized in 1859, and the town was incorporated in 1871. In 1873, both the Colorado Central and the Denver & Boulder Valley railroads arrived in town, and Boulder City's population exploded.

The first eager students arrived at Boulder's new University of Colorado campus in 1876, the same year Colorado became a state. That campus, as well as adjacent Pearl Street, is a vibrant center of activity. The area between Pearl Street and the university was once the route of a narrow-gauge railroad nicknamed the Switzerland Trail that chugged up Boulder Creek to serve mountain mining camps. First chartered in 1897 as the Colorado & Northwestern, its foreclosed property became the Denver, Boulder & Western just a decade later. The mainline connected Boulder to Sunset with a branch to Ward and another to Eldora. By 1921, all the track was gone.

Your first stop in Boulder should be the Boulder History Museum, located in the Harbeck-Bergheim House (1206 Euclid Avenue). Its excellent interpretive exhibits present the area's rich history and orient you to the many noteworthy sites. If you love beautifully preserved historic homes in elegant neighborhoods, plan on spending extra time in Boulder to explore the Mapleton Hill Historic District, as well as the University Hill and Whittier neighborhoods. The Chautauqua Park Historic District shelters many historic buildings, and the

Colorado Chautauqua Association (900 Baseline Road) has presented cultural and educational programs since 1898. The Downtown Historic District highlights many structures, including the Hotel Boulderado (2115 13th Street), opened on New Year's Day in 1909, and the Art Deco Boulder Theatre (2032 14th Street).

In the first years of the twentieth century, Pearl Street west of 14th Street was a peaceful thoroughfare disturbed only by a few plodding horses. Today, this area is a bustling pedestrian mall. *Denver Public Library, Western History Collection, L. C. McClure, MCC-300*

The Harbeck-Bergheim House was built in 1899 as a summer home for the Harbeck family. The Bergheims occupied the house from 1939 to 1969, when it was sold to the city of Boulder. The Boulder Historical Society moved into the structure in 1985, and it opened as the Boulder History Museum in 1987.

FIRST RUSH
Up Clear Creek

The 1858 Pikes Peak Gold Rush was not near Pikes Peak. Gold was first discovered in what is now Englewood. In that year, Montana City, the earliest ancestor of Denver, was established at the current site of Grant-Frontier Park (2190 S. Platte River Drive). It was quickly overshadowed by Auraria and St. Charles City. Denver City, established by General William Larimer, overlooked the confluence of the South Platte River and Cherry Creek. All these towns were in the area of modern Denver's Confluence Park (15th and Little Raven Street), where you can still watch the waters of Cherry Creek mingling with those of the South Platte River. Historic trolley tracks once ran through the park but were removed. The nearby REI store (1416 Platte Street) was the trolley barn for Denver's system of street railways. The Colorado Territory was carved out of the Kansas Territory in 1861; Denver became the territorial capital in 1865 and the state capital after statehood in 1876.

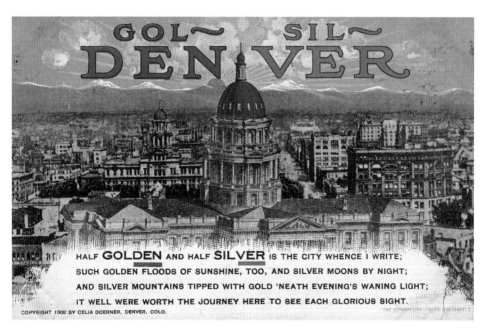

This 1910 postcard of Colorado's capitol building in Denver makes the source of the state's wealth quite clear. It was mailed to Center, Colorado, in the San Luis Valley.

DIRECTIONS

Exploration around the Denver metropolitan area will require a detailed city map. From Denver, take 44th Avenue west to the Colorado Railroad Museum. Continuing west, this road becomes Golden's 10th Street. In Golden, turn right on Washington Avenue and then west on U.S. Highway 6 through Clear Creek Canyon. Follow Colorado Highway 119 north to Blackhawk.

OPTIONAL: *Continue north on Highway 119 to cross the original Moffat railroad mainline on a bridge near Rollinsville. Immediately north of the bridge, turn left on the Rollins Pass Road for a spectacular unpaved side trip. Near the entrance to the Moffat Tunnel, turn right on Forest Road 149 (County Road 117), the old railroad grade over Rollins Pass. This road may be closed near the summit. If the road is closed and you wish to see the western half of Rollins Pass, you will have to make a very long detour via Interstate 70 and U.S. Highway 40 to reach Winter Park. At its Winter Park end, the railroad grade is the Corona Pass Road (County Road 80). Return to Blackhawk.*

In Blackhawk, head west on Gregory Street to Central City. After exploring Central City, drive south on Nevada Street, which becomes the Central City Parkway.

OPTIONAL: *To explore the Nevadaville ghost town, do not follow the Central City Parkway but turn right at the Nevadaville Road. Retrace your steps to the parkway and turn right.*

Follow signs to enter Interstate 70 westbound; take exit 241, the first exit for Idaho Springs. After exploring Idaho Springs, continue west on I-70 to exit 228 for Georgetown. You can explore Georgetown and follow the signs to the Georgetown Loop Railroad's boarding area just west of town. Return to I-70 and travel west to exit 226 for Silver Plume, where you can also board the train. Drive I-70 toward Georgetown and stop at the overlook for the Georgetown Loop Railroad, accessible only from the eastbound lanes of I-70.

The first railroad to reach Denver was the Denver Pacific in 1870, while Colorado's last major railroad, the Moffat, was completed from Denver to Craig in 1913. Denver's future was by then assured. By 1890, 107,000 souls called Denver home, making it the second-largest western metropolis after San Francisco. The "Queen City of the Plains" became a manufacturing and distribution center for both mining and agriculture.

Today downtown Denver is a forest of skyscrapers, but old Denver can still be glimpsed west of downtown in the Larimer Square Historic District (between 14th and 15th streets and from Market to Lawrence streets), a hub of shopping and nightlife. Other interesting locations are the Colorado History Museum (1300 Broadway), the Paramount Theatre (1621 Glenarm Place), the Brown Palace Hotel (321 17th Street), Trinity United Methodist Church (1820 Broadway), the Governor's Residence at the Boettcher Mansion (400 East 8th Avenue), the Colorado State Capitol (200 East Colfax Avenue), the Molly Brown House (1340 Pennsylvania Street), the Black American West Museum (3091 California Street), the Denver Firefighters Museum (1326 Tremont Place),

The elegant lobby of Denver's 1892 Brown Palace Hotel was a sedate location for this photograph, taken about the time of World War I. The hotel still welcomes guests. *Denver Public Library, Western History Collection, L. C. McClure, MCC-2401*

Four Mile Historic Park (715 South Forest Street), and the Byers-Evans House Museum (1310 Bannock Street). Denver's suburbs host the Littleton Historical Museum (6028 South Gallup Street) and the Aurora History Museum (northwest corner of Alameda and Chambers on Alameda Drive).

During the 1859 Pikes Peak Gold Rush, Golden was established where Clear Creek pours out of the mountains. It was briefly the capital of the Colorado Territory, from 1862 to 1867. Golden's commanding position at the mouth of Clear Creek's canyon made it the natural supply center for that first gold rush. W. A. H. Loveland had grander ideas, though, and chartered the Colorado Central Railroad in 1861 with the hope that a route could be found up Clear Creek to the Pacific Ocean. Though Colorado Central trains never whiffed the salt air of the Pacific, they would reach the Clear Creek mining camps. Construction of this first mountain railroad in the territory began from Golden in 1872. It is fitting that the Colorado Railroad Museum (17155 West 44th Avenue), one of the nation's finest, is also located in Golden.

A brewery, the Adolph Coors Company (13th and Ford streets), was founded by its namesake in 1873 and offers tours. In 1874, the Colorado School of Mines began its mission in Golden. Downtown Golden features historic structures that include the territorial capitol building (1122 Washington Avenue). Stop at the Golden Pioneer Museum (923 10th Street).

The Coors Brewery in Golden still receives ingredients and ships beer by the trainload, though it no longer uses antique wooden refrigerator cars like this one displayed at Golden's Colorado Railroad Museum.

Metallic gold, called placer gold, was discovered in the streams near Denver, having been washed down from its original source in the mountains. Miners headed west looking for the source of wealth, the mother lode. In 1859, prospector John Gregory discovered a golden vein along North Clear Creek between what would become Central City and Blackhawk. The Colorado Central Railroad arrived in Blackhawk in 1872. It took six long years, two switchbacks, and a trestle that flew trains across Blackhawk's main streets before the steam cars reached Central City, which was only one mile away! By 1900, though, about three thousand people lived in Central City.

The end of the authentic Wild West and the beginning of its preservation collided on a July day in 1932. The Central City Opera House was reopened in

CENTRAL CITY AREA

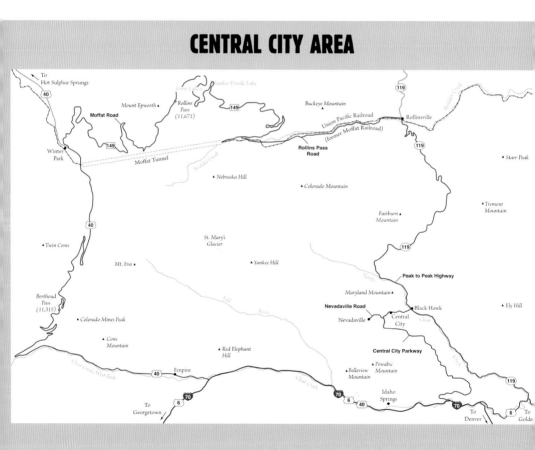

The Gilpin Gold Mill is on Colorado Highway 119 just north of Blackhawk. A dual-gauge railroad yard near this spot allowed transfers between the three-foot-gauge Colorado Central that led to Denver and the two-foot-gauge Gilpin Tram that served mines, mills, and towns in the district.

all its gold-rush grandeur. Elegant patrons traveled from Denver to Blackhawk on the last narrow-gauge passenger train to snake up Clear Creek.

Recently, legalized gambling has returned to Blackhawk and Central City, greatly altering their historic character. Nevertheless, the Central City Opera House (124 Eureka Street) and other historic buildings still stand. Visit the Gilpin History Museum (228 High Street) and explore the unpaved roads south of Central City to find ghost towns and old mines

North of Blackhawk, trains of the Union Pacific Railroad still pass through the six-mile-long Moffat tunnel. You can drive the unpaved road that was the original alignment of the Moffat railroad over the 11,660-foot Rollins Pass, the most spectacular abandoned railroad location in the United States. Drive up the loops of the Giant's Ladder, past Yankee Doodle Lake and to Needle's Eye Tunnel, where the tracks hugged the edge of a 700-foot cliff.

The 1865 date on the Rocky Mountain Lodge No. 2 of I. O. O. F. Cemetery—near Russell Gulch southwest of Central City—indicates that fatal mine accidents began to occur not long after gold was discovered. Safety was a minor concern; mine, railroad, and mill owners were often more worried about the well-being of their property than the personal safety of their employees.

The Masonic Block was a commercial building constructed in 1879 at Nevadaville, southwest of Central City. The substantial brick structure in this small, remote community is evidence of the wealth dug from the earth and the optimism that followed.

Of the abandoned railroad passes in Colorado, the route over Rollins Pass is surely the most spectacular. This dirt road is the old Rollins Pass railroad grade, and you can barely make out the entrance to the six-mile-long Moffat Tunnel at lower left.

Past the tunnel was the summit station of Corona, a small city covered by snowsheds to protect it from heavy snow. Trains descending the west side completed a loop with the upper track on a trestle precariously balanced over a tunnel through which the lower track ran. You can still find pieces of a huge steam locomotive that made the unfortunate decision to attempt flight along the loop. Check locally for conditions, but Needle's Eye Tunnel remained closed in 2008. To navigate the western portion of Rollins Pass, retrace your steps and circle around to Winter Park, where the old railroad grade can be followed eastward.

Prospectors did not stop their search with John Gregory's gold discovery. Also in 1859, George Jackson trudged up the main fork of Clear Creek and discovered gold at the present location of Idaho Springs. Though local mining was an important industry, the small metropolis would have a more important role in moving extracted wealth from the mountains north to Central City. Samuel Newhouse began promoting the construction of the Newhouse Tunnel in 1893. Its only practical purposes would be to drain water from the deepening mines to the north and to provide an inexpensive haulage route for ore. Not completed until 1910, the tunnel only briefly served those purposes. The Argo Mill was built in 1914 near the tunnel's exit. With the boom already declining, the mill

Before Elks Lodge 607 was constructed in Idaho Springs in 1907, this site was home to a hotel.

ceased to process ore within a decade. The tunnel is now called the Argo Tunnel, and you can view its entrance as part of the Argo Gold Mine and Mill tour (2350 Riverside Drive) on the east side of Idaho Springs. A walk around downtown is a wonderful experience; be sure to stop at the small Underhill Museum (1416 Miner Street). The larger Heritage Museum (2400 Colorado Boulevard), located at the visitors' center across Clear Creek from the Argo Gold Mine and Mill, includes a unique exhibit on the Clear Creek watershed and an interactive map of Colorado's mineral belt, the area that hosted most of the state's precious-metal mines. The Heritage Museum and Argo Mill tour are good starts for those new to Colorado's mining heritage.

The entrance to the Argo Tunnel is on the other side of the Argo Mill building in Idaho Springs. Water tainted by the cumulative drainage of the mines of the Clear Creek Mining District beneath Central City is routed through the Argo Tunnel to a treatment plant before being discharged into Clear Creek.

Pushing farther up the main fork of Clear Creek in 1859, the Griffith Brothers discovered gold at the location that became Georgetown. Georgetown was incorporated in 1868, and Colorado Central trains reached the town in 1877, when the town's population peaked at around five thousand. Silver, first discovered in 1864, replaced gold as Georgetown's primary source of prosperity. The era of mining ended with the repeal of the Sherman Silver Purchase Act in 1893, and the town's slow death began. Georgetown's population dipped to a few hundred in the 1930s.

Having avoided the conflagrations that destroyed many mining towns, Georgetown is packed with exceptionally old historic buildings. Besides viewing the exteriors of many beautifully restored private residences, you also can tour the Hamill House (305 Argentine Street), the Hotel de Paris Museum (409 6th Street), and the Georgetown Energy Museum (600 Griffith Street)—a hydroelectric plant that still contributes electricity. Don't miss the Alpine Hose Company No. 2 (507 5th Street), a fire station with a unique lookout tower.

The Georgetown–Silver Plume Historic District encompasses both towns, as well as the Georgetown Loop Historic Mining and Railroad Park that connects them. Many mines were actually at or above Silver Plume, where trains arrived in 1884. The elevation difference between these towns was so extreme that the railroad was forced to build more than 4 miles of track to cover 1 mile of distance—a track that included three hairpin turns and the 300-foot-long, 100-foot-high Devil's Gate Viaduct, which carried the railroad over itself on a spiral of track. The railroad and its gargantuan bridge were dismantled in 1939 but have since been restored so that you can ride over the loop once again and tour the Lebanon Mine at a stop along the way. The railroad's shops and a historic depot are in Silver Plume. Visitors can board at either Georgetown or Silver Plume.

An overlook between Silver Plume and Georgetown—accessible only to east-bound traffic on I-70—affords a panoramic view of the loop as well as some faint switchbacks in the trees on the mountainside across the valley. These switchbacks are the beginning of the Argentine Central Railway grade, which tied Silver Plume to the 11,000-foot-high silver mine at Waldorf. Built by Methodist minister Edward Wilcox in 1905, the Argentine Central never ran on Sunday. As mining declined, tourism was encouraged. Awestruck passengers could transfer from standard- to narrow-gauge cars at Denver Union Station and snake

One of the boom towns that served Colorado's first gold rush was Georgetown, established in 1859. Many of its oldest buildings are still standing, as it is one of the few historic mining towns that escaped a destructive fire.

up the canyon of Clear Creek to Silver Plume. Argentine Central locomotives would take over for the final struggle all the way to the 13,587-foot elevation of McClellan Mountain's summit, a miraculous experience for a vacationing flat-lander from the Midwest

A Shay-type geared locomotive waits for sightseers at the summit of McClellan Mountain on the Argentine Central Railway. Geared locomotives were required to traverse the sharp curves and steep grades of mountain tracks. The train's passengers are about to enter the Ice Palace, a cavern permanently encrusted with frozen water. The summits in the distance are Mt. Evans and Mt. Rosalie. *Denver Public Library, Western History Collection, L. C. McClure, MCC-697*

Reverend Sheldon Jackson established the First Presbyterian Church in Georgetown in 1869. The present stone building was completed in 1874. On October 3, 2004, a major restoration of the building was celebrated along with 130 years of continuous service to the community.

SOUTH PARK AND MORE
From Morrison to Fairplay

The discovery of dinosaur fossils near Morrison in 1877 ignited Colorado's most unusual "rush"—not a mad dash for precious metals but a frenzy for dinosaur fossils. Many fossils were eventually discovered in much of Colorado and the adjoining states. Visit Dinosaur Ridge Exhibit Hall (16831 West Alameda Parkway). Morrison also has a small downtown of wonderful old historic buildings that became a National Register Historic District in 1976.

The tranquil, rustic town of Pine once bustled with activity in a railroad yard west of the highway. Buffalo Creek was established in 1877 along the route of that same South Park railroad. Behind the J. W. Greene Mercantile Co. store (17706 County Road 96) rest some oddly angled long buildings which were warehouses flanked by sidings of the railroad. Goods from railroad cars were unloaded directly into the warehouses to supply the residents of the Buffalo Creek region. Search for the foundation of the railroad's water tank along the old railroad grade, now the unpaved South Platte River Road leading east from town. Continue east on this unpaved road to the ghost town of South Platte, where an old hotel still stands. South Platte was a summer resort, one of many that lined the railroad tracks in the refreshing mountain air west of the blistering flatlands.

Marginally financed—as were many of Colorado's railroads—the South Park halted westward construction at Morrison for four years while it gathered strength. Here, a trainload of lime rock starts a journey at Morrison that will take it to the Argo Smelter. The train is actually a mixed train, carrying freight and also passengers in the coach, which stands in front of the depot. *Colorado Historical Society, A. Neal, CHS.X4952*

DIRECTIONS

Start your journey in Morrison, just west of Denver. Southbound Colorado Highway 8 will take you to a junction with U.S. Highway 285. Go west into the mountains. Turn left at Colorado Highway 126 to pass through Pine to Buffalo Creek.

> **OPTIONAL:** *Travel east on the unpaved South Platte River Road, County Road 96, that passes in front of the J. W. Greene general store in Buffalo Creek. Arrive at South Platte, where the hotel building still stands. Return to Buffalo Creek and turn right on Highway 126.*

Retrace your route back to U.S. 285 and continue west though Bailey into South Park. To reach Como, turn right on the Boreas Pass Road, Forest Road 404. Continue on the unpaved Boreas Pass Road to Breckenridge. Immediately beyond Rotary Snowplow Park, turn right on Colorado Highway 9 to explore Breckenridge. Return south on Highway 9 to crest Hoosier Pass and arrive in Alma and then Fairplay,

> **ALTERNATE:** *If you prefer to stay on pavement, continue west from Como on U.S. 285 to reach Fairplay. Turn right on Highway 9 to explore Fairplay, reach Alma, escape South Park over Hoosier Pass, and arrive in Breckenridge.*

The J. W. Greene general store at Buffalo Creek was once the source of supplies for the region. The long warehouse buildings behind the store were served by sidings of the South Park railroad.

THE DENVER, SOUTH PARK & PACIFIC RAILROAD

IN A STATE ONCE CROWDED with spectacular railroads, most of which were founded on wildly optimistic hopes of profit, two railroads stand out. These are the Rio Grande Southern (Journey 14) and the Denver, South Park & Pacific. The South Park, as it was called, crested five mountain passes—three more than eleven-thousand feet above sea level—all the while searching for a place to go. It wandered this way and that but always arrived as the gold rush, silver rush, or coal-mining boom was just ending!

John Evans began construction of the South Park in Denver, hoping to provide mountain access for the Queen City of the Plains. With marginal financing, the South Park's construction stalled at Morrison in 1874, just a few miles west of Denver. Leadville's riches inspired the resumption of construction in 1878, and trains arrived in Como in 1879. The boom at Fairplay had already turned into a whimper, however, so the tracks continued over Trout Creek Pass to connect with the Denver & Rio Grande near Buena Vista and share its narrow-gauge track into Leadville. In return, the Rio Grande's trains would be allowed to travel to Gunnison through the South Park's Alpine Tunnel, at that time still a dream in a promoter's eye. By the time the South Park reached Gunnison in 1882, ownership of both lines had changed and agreements for joint use of tracks had been cancelled.

As a consequence, the South Park built another high-altitude line that topped Boreas Pass to provide itself access to Leadville (Journey 10), while the Rio Grande built its own track over Marshall Pass to reach Gunnison (Journey 11). Narrow-gauge railroads were constructed with their rails closer together than the standard gauge of 4 feet, 8 ½ inches. Most Colorado narrow-gauge railroads were built with 3 feet between the rails. These lines were also built with steeper gradients and tighter curves than were common on standard-gauge railroads. All these attributes made narrow-gauge railroad construction much less expensive, especially in the mountains, where earthwork was most costly. Smaller locomotives and cars also made these railroads less expensive to equip. Their fatal weakness was that narrow-gauge railroad cars could not be directly interchanged with the majority of U.S. railroads.

The last narrow-gauge train between Denver and Leadville ran in 1937, while narrow-gauge trains continued to connect Leadville to the molybdenum mine at Climax until 1943, when that line was converted to standard width. Freight trains of the Burlington Northern continued running to Climax until 1986; that same track is now the passenger-hauling Leadville, Colorado & Southern.

A Denver, South Park & Pacific train follows the South Platte River in 1923. *Library of Congress, Keystone View Company, LC-USZ62-118085*

Retrace your steps back to U.S. Highway 285 and continue west to reach Bailey. The Bailey family arrived in this isolated mountain location in 1864, establishing a ranch and a stage stop on their property. Fourteen years later, the South Park railroad reached the town of Bailey, and a post office opened. Today, McGraw Park offers a five-acre self-guided tour of several historic buildings, some from the 1864 founding of the town.

At Como, the South Park mainline from Denver split into two routes. The first traveled southwest to a junction with the Fairplay branch, over Trout Creek Pass, up Chalk Creek to St. Elmo, and through the Continental Divide at Alpine Tunnel to reach Gunnison (Journey 11). The second headed northwest to cross the Continental Divide over Boreas Pass, reaching Breckenridge; circled south to Climax, crossing the Continental Divide a second time over Fremont Pass; and ended its trek at Leadville. Day and night, toy-like trains bustled around the Como yard. Even short trains might require as many as four locomotives to lift them over these three crossings of the Continental Divide.

The six original stone stalls of the South Park roundhouse still stand at Como. Another dozen wooden stalls are long gone. The short turntable in the foreground was adequate to turn the tiny locomotives that challenged the Continental Divide at three separate crossings.

In 1910, the tracks over Boreas Pass, over Trout Creek Pass, and through the Alpine Tunnel were closed. The Boreas Pass line reopened in a few years, and trains hauled ore from Leadville through Como to Denver as late as 1937. Nevertheless, Como was doomed. A peak population of 350 decayed to a tenth of that number by 1911. Imagine three dozen lonely people stranded in this frigid, remote town with a dying railroad, just waiting for their employment to end. The six original stone stalls of what was once an eighteen-stall railroad roundhouse (the other twelve were wooden) still stand, and restoration is slowly proceeding. The depot is also still here, as are Como's old school house and many antique residences.

The unpaved route over Boreas Pass will take you past Robert's Cabin, a rustic residence built in the 1880s and now available for overnight lodging. At Rocky Point, where the railroad grade and road diverge for a short distance, the Forest Service has laid narrow-gauge track with volunteer help. The 1882 section house at the summit has recently been rebuilt with the assistance of volunteers. The section gang—workers who maintained the track over the Boreas Pass summit—lived here. As you travel down the north side of the pass, you'll encounter the restored Bakers Tank, where steam locomotives quenched their thirst. Arriving in Breckenridge, the centerpiece of Rotary Snow Plow Park (French Street and the Boreas Pass Road) is a railroad snowplow along with a small interpretive exhibit.

One of the major railroad artifacts on Boreas Pass is Bakers Tank. Water tanks like this once dotted all the rail lines in Colorado but were either reclaimed with the demise of the railroad or destroyed by Colorado's heavy snowfalls. Bakers Tank survives only because it is maintained by those who want history preserved.

This mine is near the location of Buckskin Joe just west of Alma. Here, beautiful Silver Heels ministered to the miners who became victims of a smallpox epidemic.

Prospectors scouted the Breckenridge area in 1859 as opportunities on Clear Creek (Journey 7) became scarce. Gold was discovered, and Breckenridge was established to serve the mines and miners in the area. The town is chock full of history. Visit the 1880 Alice G. Milne House (102 North Harris Street) on a walking tour of the National Historic District of Breckenridge. The 1875 Edwin Carter Museum (111 South Ridge Street) is the second oldest in the state and includes general information about the history of the town. The Breckenridge Heritage Alliance sponsors interpretive tours of numerous sites in the Breckenridge area, including the Washington Mine and Lomax Placer Gulch. The Country Boy Mine hosts tours, as well.

You can also see Father Dyer's Cabin (310 Wellington Road) in Breckenridge. John Dyer, a Methodist minister, arrived in Denver in 1861. He founded a church in Breckenridge in 1880, when he was sixty-eight years old. He is most famous for circuit-riding via cross-country skis (then called Norwegian snowshoes) among churches at Alma, Fairplay, and Leadville. Dyer, in his late sixties, trekked between Alma and Leadville, cresting 13,186-foot Mosquito Pass in mid-winter.

Almost nothing is left of the town of Buckskin Joe, just west of Alma on an unpaved road, but the legend of a beautiful woman called Silver Heels will likely keep the town alive if only in memories. A smallpox epidemic attacked the mining camp in 1861, and Silver Heels spent arduous hours nursing the sick. Many died, as the epidemic lasted for months. Silver Heels—by some accounts an entertainer and by others a prostitute—vanished. The legend says that she contracted the deadly disease, and her lovely face was scarred for life. Several years after the epidemic, a heavily veiled woman thought to be Silver Heels was seen in the Buckskin Joe cemetery adorning graves with flowers.

Founded in 1859, Fairplay was also one of Colorado's first precious-metal towns. It is the largest town in the 900-square-mile, 8,500-foot-high mountain-rimmed basin called South Park. Tour South Park City (Main and Fourth Streets), an outdoor living-history museum where many nineteenth-century mountain mining camp buildings and tens of thousands of artifacts have been collected. The steam locomotive displayed in the museum compound is not a South Park loco, but it is very similar to those that once steamed up the branch to Fairplay. It will give you a sense of just how small these locomotives were. Imagine four of these "teapots" pushing the rotary snowplow displayed in Breckenridge to the summit of Boreas Pass.

BIG BANDS TO TRANSCONTINENTALS
Along the Platte River Road

The Overland Trail, which in Colorado largely followed the South Platte River, was one of the most heavily traveled of the emigrant trails. Fort Morgan was built in 1864 and 1865 to protect those emigrants and the U.S. mail from Indian attack. In 1867, the Union Pacific constructed a rail line across Wyoming, parallel to the Overland Trail, ending the latter's usefulness and closing Fort Morgan. The area's future changed dramatically in 1882, when the Burlington Railroad completed a line that connected Denver with the Midwest and passed near old Fort Morgan. It is no surprise that Abner Baker created a town site here just a year later. The city of Fort Morgan was incorporated in 1887.

Two small locomotives are displayed at Fort Morgan. Tiny locomotives like these switched railroad cars at Great Western Sugar plants all over Colorado, and many are on display. The City of Fort Morgan Power Plant building now houses the city's parks department.

DIRECTIONS

N
W E
S

Your journey starts in Fort Morgan, east of Denver on Interstate 76. The Fort Morgan Museum is in the library on Main Street, south of exit 80. Continue east on I-76. Sterling's Overland Trail Museum is near exit 125, where U.S. Highway 6 intersects I-76. Travel east on I-76 to exit 172 and then north to Ovid. Turn right on U.S. Highway 138. The Great Western Sugar plant will be on your right as you leave town. Follow U.S. 138; it becomes Julesburg's 1st Street, on which both of its museums are located.

The Fort Morgan Museum (414 Main Street) interprets the area's history with both images and artifacts. The soda fountain from the nearby town of Hillrose is set in a re-creation of the store in which it served soft drinks for many years. The museum does not neglect Fort Morgan's most famous musician. Glenn Miller, a graduate of Fort Morgan High School, led a band that became arguably the most famous of the Big Band era. His recording of "Chattanooga Choo Choo" was the first gold record, selling over one million copies. Though Miller was killed serving in World War II, his band continues to thrive and often plays at Fort Morgan's annual Glenn Miller Festival.

Sugar beets were a major source of agricultural wealth in Colorado, and processing plants owned by the Great Western Sugar Company dotted the state. Most, like this one at Ovid, still stand, unused reminders of a business gone bad.

The high plains around Sterling were inhabited by Arapaho, Blackfoot, Cheyenne, Crow, Kiowa, Pawnee, and Sioux Indians. The last battle between American Indians and the U.S. Army occurred at Summit Springs, just east of Sterling, on July 11, 1869. This battle, coupled with the completion of the first transcontinental railroad just a month earlier, marked the end of the era of Indians and mountain men and the beginning of U.S. settlement of the American West.

The Burlington and Union Pacific railroads intersected in Sterling, assuring its economic success. Sterling's Overland Trail Museum (U.S. Highway 6, just west of I-76 at exit 125) was established in 1933 and includes a large number of indoor and outdoor exhibits. An unusual exhibit chronicles the history of rural electrification, an expansion of technology that profoundly affected the lifestyles of the region's settlers.

Ovid is a prime example of the effect that the Great Western Sugar Company and its demise had on Colorado. Most of Colorado's sugar-beet industry developed on its eastern plains. The Great Western Sugar Company was incorporated in 1905, absorbing several existing sugar factories and expanding into Montana, Wyoming, and Nebraska. Falling sugar prices, poor management, and inadequate investment led to the 1974 sale of the company to a firm owned by the infamous Hunt brothers, members of what was once America's

Major Glenn Miller conducts the military incarnation of his civilian band during World War II at an open-air concert. Miller grew up in Fort Morgan and attended the University of Colorado at Boulder. *U.S. Air Force*

wealthiest family. Operations expanded into other states and other products, but competition from less expensive materials such as sugar cane and corn syrup adversely impacted local sugar-beet production. The Ovid plant closed in the 1980s, when local growers refused to plant sugar beets at the price offered. The Hunts filed for bankruptcy in 1987 after failed speculation in the silver market, which led to their 1988 conviction on charges of conspiracy to manipulate that market. Pieces of their sugar empire were parceled out to other companies. Today, the Western Sugar Cooperative processes sugar beets at Fort Morgan and in plants in surrounding states.

Julesburg is a city of transportation and communication: the Overland Trail, the Pony Express, the transcontinental telegraph, and the transcontinental railroad all passed through or near the town. In 1859, Jules Beni was hired as a station-keeper for the Overland Stage Company and settled near what became the first of several town sites named Julesburg. Beni was involved in mail tampering, assault, cattle rustling, and other "harmless" hobbies. He was finally killed in a quasi-legal execution in 1861.

The Union Pacific depot at Julesburg is now one of two museums in town. Here, the first transcontinental railroad just nicked the state of Colorado in 1867.

Fort Sedgwick was erected at Julesburg in 1864 to protect emigrant wagon trains, as well as the transcontinental telegraph, which had replaced the Pony Express within just *two days* of the telegraph's completion in 1861. Fort Sedgwick was abandoned in 1871 after conflicts with Indians ended. That was not the end of Julesburg, though, for the town had become a stop on the new transcontinental railroad. The current Julesburg is the fourth location of that town in this vicinity. Two museums—the Fort Sedgwick Museum (114 East 1st Street) and the Depot Museum (201 West 1st Street)—entice the visitor with local history and some of the most helpful volunteers in Colorado.

Though Holyoke is located between Journey 9 and Journey 19, it's home to the splendid Phillips County Museum, which features these two antique gas pumps. Gasoline was pumped into the glass canisters at the top of the pumps to assure the customer that the correct amount was being dispensed. The liquid energy would then run down a hose, drawn by gravity into the automobile's gasoline tank.

CENTRAL COLORADO
The Mountain Middle

COLORADO'S MOUNTAIN MIDDLE is central to the state's mining and railroad history. Much of this area has remained relatively unscathed by modern development, so you can still experience the ambiance of Colorado's early history.

As in much of Colorado, the railroad's presence influenced the development of the land. The Arkansas River was one of the easiest routes to Colorado's mountainous interior, so it is no surprise that it was chosen as the route for the Denver & Rio Grande Railroad, which continued over Tennessee Pass and down the valley of the Eagle River, a tributary of the mighty Colorado. A much more difficult task was accessing the Gunnison River on the other side of the Continental Divide. Nevertheless, two railroads managed to arrive at the banks of the Gunnison; one actually descended into the depths of the Black Canyon, carved out by that river. Both railroads were narrow gauge, a backwater technology that doomed this area to a remoteness that helped preserve its history.

Both slopes of the Continental Divide feature pastoral landscapes that supported farming and ranching as well as rocky terrain that was often the province of mining. Precious-metal mines generated wealth, and Leadville has the most and the best preserved historic structures of the ostentatious towns that such wealth created. Coal mining was not as lucrative, so you'll find Crested Butte smaller and less grand, though the spectacular mountain valley in which it lies may compensate.

This picturesque highway bridge straddles the Eagle River gorge above a smaller road bridge. At the bottom of the "stack" is the railroad over Tennessee Pass. A precipitous road leads from the northern end of the high bridge into secluded Red Cliff, which you can leave on Water Street via the lower bridge, crossing the railroad tracks to rejoin the main highway.

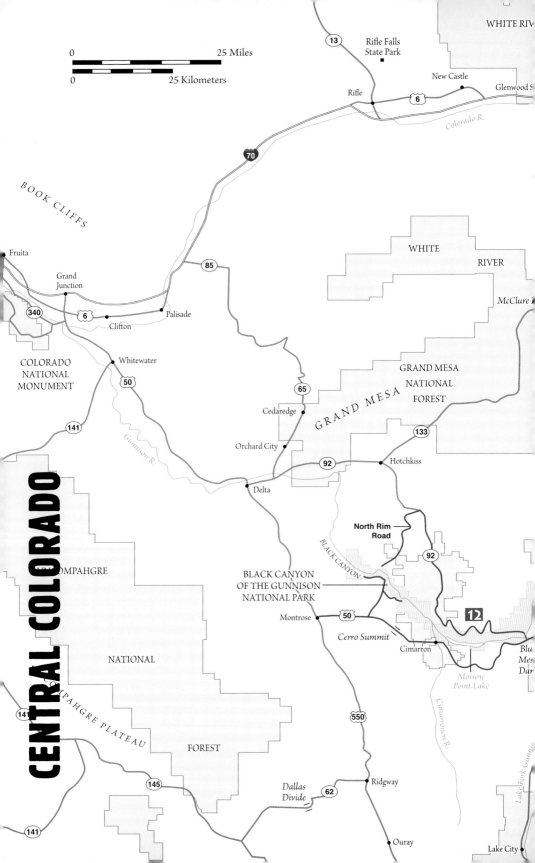

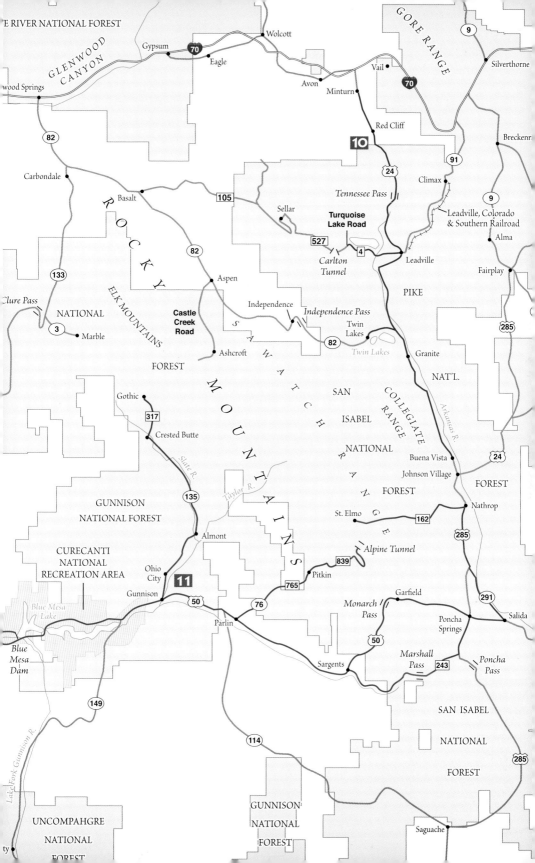

THE HIGH LIFE
East of the Divide

Minturn boomed in 1887 as a helper station for Denver & Rio Grande trains struggling up Tennessee Pass, currently the highest mainline railroad in North America (though it is closed with no plans to reopen). Westbound trains would drop extra locomotives here, where they were serviced and then used to help eastbound trains over the pass. When steam locomotives ruled the rails, Minturn hosted a roundhouse complete with a turntable for spinning 120-foot-long locos end for end. The railroad facilities were east of the highway on the north side of town. One interesting historical remnant remains: the Turntable Restaurant (160 Railroad Avenue). Such "beaneries" were common near all railroad yards. Few are left, but the Turntable Restaurant is still in its original location dishing out meals, even if no longer primarily to railroad workers.

Your first glimpse of Gilman is quite unexpected: It is a large, intact ghost town perched on a steep slope adjacent to U.S. Highway 24. The settlement was established in 1879 and was known as Clinton until 1886. Gold, sliver, lead, copper, and zinc were all eventually mined here. The Eagle Mine, which consolidated small independent producers in the area, was open from 1912 to 1977. Gilman was closed to the public in 1984 because it is private property and is contaminated by hazardous waste from mining operations.

Farther along, hidden in the Eagle River gorge, is Red Cliff, established in the 1870s. The arrival of the railroad fueled its growth and the mines it served. A popular sidetrip connects Red Cliff with I-70 via the Shrine Pass road, which is suitable for four-wheel-drive vehicles.

Camp Hale was established in 1942 for winter mountain warfare training. Up to sixteen thousand soldiers, including the Tenth Mountain Division, trained here during World War II. The training site was colossal, extending from just south of Red Cliff to just north of Leadville and encompassing almost a quarter-million acres. Soldiers arrived by train and lived in the flat valley of Eagle Park. The camp was deactivated in 1965; portions remain closed due to ongoing efforts to clean up munitions left on the property. Much of the site is open to the public, however. You can glimpse foundations and some remains of concrete structures in Eagle Park or learn more about Camp Hale from an interpretive display.

DIRECTIONS

Minturn is on U.S. Highway 24, just south of Interstate Highway 70 exit 171. Follow U.S. 24 south through Leadville to Buena Vista.

OPTIONAL: *To hike to Hagerman Tunnel, go west on Leadville's 6th Street, the Turquoise Lake Road. Bear left at Forest Road 105 almost at the western end of Turquoise Lake. You'll pass the Carlton Tunnel (formerly the Busk-Ivanhoe Tunnel) just before the trail parking area. Inquire locally for detailed directions and allow a good portion of a day.*

In addition to the need for consistently large amounts of snow, the winter-warfare training site of Camp Hale was chosen for road and rail access. The Tennessee Pass line of the Denver & Rio Grande brought construction materials, supplies, troops, and even animals to this remote location. Some of the camp's many buildings in Eagle Park appear in the background.
Denver Public Library, Western History Collection, William A. Southworth, Z-5346

An antique fire engine stands guard outside the modern Leadville fire department. Leadville was one of the few Colorado mining towns never to suffer a calamitous fire, accounting for the continued existence of many of its oldest structures.

Soon the highway crests Tennessee Pass at 10,424 feet. The trains chugged through a tunnel below the highway at a mere 10,200 feet. Oro City appeared at this locale sometime in the 1860s to serve a boomlet of gold mining in the area. Heavy black sand impeded gold recovery and nearly ended the future industrialization here until 1876, when it was discovered that the sand contained large amounts of silver. Leadville, the best preserved of Colorado's large, prosperous, mining boom towns, was born in 1877. The ensuing silver boom was magnificent, with three railroads, an opera house, a large commercial district, and even a short-lived street railway serving the town. Who would have believed that all this would suddenly appear at 10,152 feet above sea level?

Leadville was Colorado's second largest metropolis by 1892. Only Denver was larger. Unfortunately, the boom ended almost as quickly as it had begun with the 1893 repeal of the Sherman Silver Purchase Act.

It was in Leadville where wealthy merchant Horace Tabor infamously left his wife, Augusta Tabor, for young and beautiful Elizabeth McCourt Doe in 1880. He married "Baby Doe" in 1882, but that marriage was not legalized until 1883 since Augusta had contested their divorce. Horace's fortunes declined with those of Leadville. He would have ended his life as a three-dollar-a-day laborer but was appointed postmaster of Leadville just a year before his death in 1899. Baby Doe died in 1935 at the Matchless Mine—once one of Tabor's wealth-spewing holdings—where she lived in a shack through the generosity of the mine's owner. You can tour the surface plant of the Matchless Mine and Baby Doe Tabor's last home (1 1/4 miles east of Harrison on 7th Street).

Leadville is crowded with historic buildings, both commercial and residential. A long visit is worthwhile. As a newly minted millionaire whose fortunes hadn't yet turned, Horace Tabor constructed Leadville's Tabor Opera House (308 Harrison Avenue) in 1879. You should not miss touring its elaborate interior. There are also several museums, including the Heritage Museum (102 East 9th Street), the National Mining Hall of Fame and Museum (120 West 9th Street), and the Healy House and Dexter Cabin Museum (912 Harrison Avenue). The Leadville, Colorado & Southern Railroad (326 East 7th Street) carries passengers to Climax on the historic South Park rail line.

The first production at Leadville's Tabor Opera House opened on November 20, 1879. Most so-called "opera houses" of the American West seldom hosted operas but were venues for civic events, band concerts, and plays. *Denver Public Library, Western History Collection, Alfred Brisbois, X-180*

The molybdenum mine at Climax closed in 1987, at which time the railroad connecting the mine with Leadville became the passenger-hauling Leadville, Colorado & Southern Railroad.

The Colorado Midland Railway was the first standard-gauge railroad to challenge Colorado's mountains and one of three that served Leadville. Trains were projected to arrive on the shores of the Pacific Ocean but never even reached Colorado's border with Utah. Construction started from Colorado Springs in 1886, and the Midland's tracks arrived in Glenwood Springs in 1887. A track jointly owned with the Denver & Rio Grande completed its route to Grand Junction. The Colorado Midland was built quickly because other railroads along its route could deliver supplies and because the construction of those railroads had pioneered knowledge of the lay of Colorado's mountain lands. Unfortunately, these circumstances also meant that the Colorado Midland was the last railroad to arrive at most of its destinations and had to spend more money to lay its tracks in less desirable places. It ceased operations in 1918, and most of its rails were removed in 1921.

Flumes were used to transport water for mining, agriculture, and domestic use. Abandoned railroad grades crisscross the mountains and are often easy to spot, since much effort was spent to make them very flat. A grade for a flume may be difficult to distinguish from an old railroad grade if the flume itself is no longer visible.

HAGERMAN TUNNEL AREA

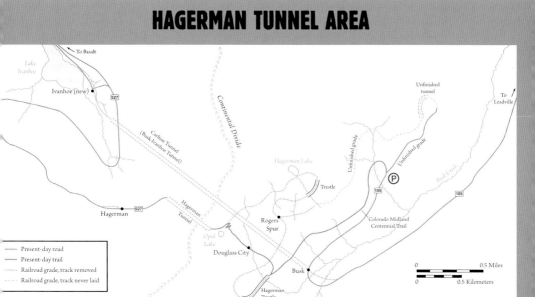

This railroad's legacy is one of the most beautiful and historic day hikes in Colorado, up the east side of Hagerman Pass, west of Leadville. On the Colorado Midland Centennial Trail, you'll hike through the ghost town of Douglass City and end up at the ice-filled east portal of Hagerman Tunnel.

South of the Independence Pass road junction leading to Twin Lakes, you'll drive through a wide spot in the road named Granite, where a few buildings remain. The town originally provided access to nearby mines but was best known in its role as a facilitator for holidays. Imagine a train arriving here on either the Colorado Midland or the Denver & Rio Grande. Hordes of passengers crowd the platform while their luggage is unloaded; somehow, in this bedlam, each group of vacationers and their baggage find their way to the correct stagecoach; the train whistles away, and the stages depart for resorts on the shores of Twin Lakes. The most famous of these resorts was Interlaken on the south shore of the lake. Hikers can access the nineteenth-century structure that was once the Inter-Laken Hotel.

The Denver & Rio Grande changed Granite's name to Yale after a 1926 passenger train wreck cost the lives of thirty passengers. (Changing names was a common practice after particularly ugly wrecks.) The post office retained the name Granite, however, and the town's remains are so named today.

Stagecoaches faced challenges in the treacherous terrain as well. Many struggled to reach Aspen over Independence Pass, west of Twin Lakes. Those stages passed though Dayton, now named Twin Lakes Village, a resort town where you can view easily accessible nineteenth-century structures.

Farther downriver in the Arkansas Valley is the aptly named Buena Vista, "Good View" in Spanish. The view of the Continental Divide—here called the Collegiate Range—is particularly awe-inspiring. Buena Vista never enjoyed the wild and wooly atmosphere so common in the American West. Its origins were grounded in farming and ranching, not in mining. The Chaffee County seat was once located here after the good citizens of Buena Vista hijacked the county records from Granite in the middle of the night. The seat of county government continued to move downstream and eventually arrived in Salida, where it is located today. The county's former courthouse in Buena Vista was used as a school from 1928 to 1968. It now houses the Buena Vista Heritage Museum (506 East Main Street), which is worth visiting, as are all the unexpectedly substantial heritage structures in the old town center located east of U.S. Highway 24 on Main Street.

This small mine is found east of Highway 24 along the Brown's Canyon road between Buena Vista and Salida. This road leads to the Arkansas River, providing access for commercial river-rafting firms. Across the river is Railroad Gulch, where a railroad once served a marble quarry and a small iron mine. The mine provided raw material to the steel mill at Pueblo.

OVER AND OVER AGAIN
Crossing the Continental Divide

This journey includes two possible crossings of the Continental Divide, as well as a near third crossing blocked by a collapsed railroad tunnel.

St. Elmo is a picturesque ghost town in Chalk Creek Canyon that was officially established in 1880 to serve a mining district. Residents welcomed the Denver, South Park & Pacific Railroad in 1882 when it arrived on its way to the Alpine Tunnel, through which it scurried under the Continental Divide. The route from St. Elmo to the eastern portal of Alpine Tunnel begins on the road over Hancock Pass, suitable only for four-wheel-drive vehicles, and then requires a substantial hike to the tunnel portal. You'll prefer the western approach to the tunnel, described later in this journey, as it is more easily accessed and more interesting.

Snow was so deep along St. Elmo's railroad line that it was the location of a contest to judge the effectiveness of newly invented railroad rotary snow plows in 1890. The contest was won by the Leslie plow, which became the industry standard and is still used today. So difficult was snow removal that the Alpine Tunnel was closed permanently in 1910. (The great bore had also been closed from 1890 to 1895.) St. Elmo's population of two thousand dwindled to nothing with the loss of railroad transportation.

ALPINE TUNNEL AREA

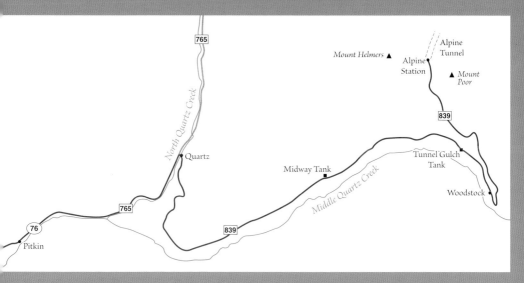

DIRECTIONS

From Nathrop on U.S. Highway 285, go west on County Road 162 to reach St. Elmo. This road is unpaved near St. Elmo but is usually negotiable in an ordinary passenger car. Return to Nathrop and turn right on U.S. 285. Turn left on Colorado Highway 291 to reach downtown Salida. Continue through Salida on Highway 291 and turn right on U.S. Highway 50 to Poncha Springs.

> **ALTERNATE:** *Continue west from Poncha Springs on U.S. 50 if you prefer to remain on paved roads and rejoin the journey at Sargents.*

Turn left on U.S. 285 and start toward Poncha Pass. Turn right on Forest Road 243, the Marshall Pass Road, and continue to Sargents. Continue west on U.S. 50. Turn right at Parlin on County Road 76 to reach Ohio City and Pitkin.

> **OPTIONAL:** *Continue though Pitkin on unpaved Forest Road 765, the Cumberland Pass Road, and turn right on Forest Road 839, the Alpine Tunnel Road. Continue to the tunnel. Return to Pitkin.*

Retrace your route to Parlin and then continue west to Gunnison on U.S. 50. Turn north on Colorado Highway 135 to reach Crested Butte.

The Denver & Rio Grande Railroad bypassed an existing town to build its own, Salida, and reaped handsome profits from doing so. Here the narrow-gauge mainline from Denver headed west over Marshall Pass to Salt Lake City. When it became obvious that narrow-gauge track was a dead-end technology, the railroad built a standard-gauge mainline following the Arkansas River through Salida to crest Tennessee Pass and reach Salt Lake City.

Salida is the Spanish word for "gateway," and Salida is indeed the gateway to the heart of Colorado's mountains. Though Salida is strongly identified as a

St. Elmo's population peaked at about two thousand during its initial mining boom, fueled by the coming of the railroad. The snow that doomed the rail line is still evident in this springtime photo.

railroad town, its first European settlers farmed and ranched, and those activities still contribute to the local economy. The town has become a center of recreational activities on the Arkansas River and in the nearby mountains. Disastrous fires in 1886 and 1888 encouraged new construction. Today many downtown commercial buildings stand as historic landmarks and havens for artists.

Much of what you can see in this historic photo still stands in Salida. Even after the standard-gauge track was built to Salt Lake City, the narrow-gauge line continued to serve local stations in western Colorado with routes up the Poncha, Marshall, and Monarch passes, all beginning with the track, which heads toward the mountains, at the right of this photo.
Denver Public Library, Western History Collection, L. C. McClure, MCC-3996

This brick smokestack climbs 365 feet skyward and is all that remains of a once substantial lead/zinc smelter operated near Salida until the 1920s. The smelter was constructed by the Ohio and Colorado Smelting and Refining Company in 1902.

Poncha Springs was platted in 1879. It had the first library in the county and was once a rival to Salida for both the county seat and the substantial railroad shops that would eventually be constructed at Salida. Here you have decision to make. If you are averse to driving unpaved roads, you can deviate from this journey and continue west over Monarch Pass. As you near the Monarch Pass summit, you'll see a large limestone quarry southwest of the small community of Garfield. Until the mid-1980s, trains carried limestone down from these lofty heights to Pueblo, where it was used as one of the key ingredients in steel-making. The track is gone and the quarry closed. Descending Monarch Pass, you'll soon encounter the western end of the Marshall Pass road at the town of Sargents.

This concrete foundation marks the location of a water tank that quenched the thirst of steam locomotives on Marshall Pass. Even where such tanks have been removed or crushed by snow, their foundation and piping may still be visible. Some tanks included nearby underground cisterns as part of their plumbing system, so be careful where you step.

If you choose unpaved Marshall Pass as your route, you'll begin to ascend Poncha Pass as narrow-gauge trains did until the mid-1950s. Part way up, after turning west on the Marshall Pass road, you can spot the location of Mears Junction, where the railroad to Alamosa diverged on a flyover—one track crossing over the other on a bridge. The only remaining evidence of this feat is an earthen fill on the south side of the road with a cut through it. One track occupied the bottom of the cut, while the other traversed the top of the fill. As you gain elevation, you'll know you're driving on the old railroad as your car travels through steep-sided earthen cuts that no one in his right mind would have excavated for a minor road. If you search near the summit, you may find the pit where a covered turntable allowed rotary snowplows to be turned in a storm, since they could not plow backwards!

Sargents was a railroad helper station, pure and simple. Here locomotives were fueled, watered, lubricated, and otherwise maintained before being added

The numerous outdoor exhibits at the Gunnison Pioneer Museum include this Denver & Rio Grande freight train complete with steam locomotive.

JOHN GUNNISON GRADUATED from West Point Military Academy, second in his class, in 1837. His early duties included participating in conflicts with Seminole Indians in Florida and exploring the wild frontier along the Michigan-Wisconsin border. An 1849 expedition to Salt Lake City saw him mediating disputes between Native Americans and Mormon settlers.

In 1853, Captain Gunnison was selected to lead an expedition to seek out possible routes for a Pacific railroad along the Kansas-Nebraska border and through Colorado. He first considered the Black Canyon where the Gunnison River joins its Lake Fork (Journey 12). After some exploration, he concluded that a route though the deep, dark canyon would not be suitable for a Pacific railroad—and Gunnison viewed only the eastern edge of the canyon, the least rugged! His party wisely bypassed the Black Canyon to reach the present site of Montrose and then proceeded into Utah.

Gunnison himself did not survive the expedition. He was murdered in October 1853 on the bank of Utah's Sevier River. Recent Paiute Indian raids on Mormon settlements suggested that members of that tribe were responsible for the attack, though there is some controversy over that conclusion. The town of Gunnison and the Gunnison River were named in remembrance of John Gunnison, honoring him for his early exploration of this region.

The formidable Gunnison River and the town of Gunnison were named after explorer Captain John Gunnison, who passed through here. Gunnison's Main Street north of Tomichi Avenue is now paved and is still the primary route to Crested Butte. Though the street no longer features horses and wagons, many historic buildings remain here.
Denver Public Library, Western History Collection, M. Brunfield, X-9394

to eastbound trains to help with the struggle over Marshall Pass. When the track over Marshall Pass was removed in the mid-1950s, Sargents was such a pristine example of a Colorado railroad town that an effort was made to preserve the entire town and its railroad facilities as a museum. This did not come to pass, but there are railroad and other historic structures still in town, including a railroad water tank, a depot building, and an old schoolhouse.

After turning northeast at Parlin, you'll be following the route of the Denver, South Park & Pacific Railroad to its Alpine Tunnel crossing through the Continental Divide. The small hamlet of Ohio City appears and disappears quickly before you arrive at the larger town of Pitkin. Founded in 1879 as a mining camp, Pitkin was briefly named Quartzville. By 1880, almost three dozen

The Denver & Rio Grande once served the Crested Butte Depot with narrow-gauge trains. Tracks were torn up in the mid-1950s. At least one proposal has been made to rebuild the railroad as far as the Gunnison airport to carry skiers to the mountain town.

mines were wresting minerals from the earth near town. Commercial loggers began felling trees to feed to a sawmill in Pitkin in 1881.

Again you have a decision. If you are not averse to dirt roads, continue through Pitkin to the western portal of the Alpine Tunnel. Though these roads are unpaved, they may be passable in ordinary passenger cars. Be warned that the last part of the Alpine Tunnel road is not for those squeamish about heights.

Thirteen people were killed when the town of Woodstock was obliterated in a March 1884 avalanche. A passenger train had just passed though Woodstock and began to circle around to climb the track behind the town. Imagine the horror when the passengers of that train actually *witnessed* the thundering mass of white death that destroyed the town and took thirteen lives. Alpine Station stands near the western portal of this 11,460-foot-high railroad tunnel, which was completed in 1882.

Gunnison came to life in the 1870s with the rise of mining all over Colorado. The Denver & Rio Grande chugged into town in 1881 via Marshall Pass, and the Denver, South Park & Pacific arrived two years later though the Alpine Tunnel. However, by 1883 the prospects of precious-metal mining in the area had plummeted, and Gunnison settled down to a long history of ranching and coal mining. Home to Western State College and gateway to the Crested Butte ski area, its economy was fed by education and recreation. Unlike many towns in this situation, Gunnison has retained its historic ambiance. As you enter the town, you'll see the substantial outdoor displays of the Gunnison Pioneer Museum (803 East Tomichi Avenue) on the south side of the highway. Be sure to stop here to take a pleasant outdoor walk and to view the indoor exhibits, which will orient you to the area's history.

North of Gunnison, you'll follow the Taylor River to the tiny hamlet of Almont, after which the highway clings to the tributary Slate River all the way to Crested Butte. Placer mines first appeared in the region in the 1860s, and silver was the precious metal unearthed here. Small deposits and the 1893 repeal of the Sherman Silver Purchase Act would have doomed the region except for an active coal-mining industry and the supply needs of area ranches. Coal mining declined and finally ceased after the last local railroad ripped up its steel trail in the mid-1950s. Crested Butte, smaller and more remote than Gunnison, declined into the category of ghost town until skiing revitalized it as a center first of winter and then of summer recreation. The Crested Butte Mountain Heritage Museum (331 Elk Avenue) also hosts the Mountain Bike Hall of Fame and Museum.

North of Crested Butte is the town of Gothic, owned by the Rocky Mountain Biological Laboratory since 1928. Besides hosting researchers, the laboratory offers educational programs suitable for a wide variety of visitors. The road continues over Schofield Pass, but travel all the way to Marble is not advised unless you are a very experienced four-wheel-drive enthusiast. Parts of the road between Gothic and Marble are considered the most dangerous in Colorado, and many fatalities have occurred along this route.

North of Crested Butte is the town of Gothic, born of silver mining in 1879. By the 1920s, it had become a ghost town. Since 1928, it has been home to the Rocky Mountain Biological Laboratory. *Denver Public Library, Western History Collection, George Beam, GB-8364*

DEEP AND STEEP
Into the Black Canyon

There are three reservoirs west of Gunnison: Blue Mesa, Morrow Point, and Crystal. All are included in the Curecanti National Recreation Area. The Gunnison River was dammed to create these bodies of water as that river descended through the Black Canyon. The rim around the canyon attracted ancient cultures with its copious natural resources, while the depths of the canyon were ignored as an inhospitable barrier.

Blue Mesa Dam created Blue Mesa Reservoir and also carries Colorado Highway 92 on the most scenic approach to the north rim of Back Canyon in Gunnison National Park.

DIRECTIONS

Travel west from Gunnison on U.S. Highway 50 through Cimarron to reach the entrance to Black Canyon of the Gunnison National Park and Montrose.

OPTIONAL: *If you wish to visit the park's north rim, turn right on Colorado Highway 92 to reach Crawford and follow the signs for the unpaved North Rim Road. The north rim excursion will require a long day. Return to U.S. 50 and turn right to reach Montrose.*

As you travel west along the shore of Blue Mesa Reservoir, you arrive at a small town named Sapinero. This is actually *new* Sapinero, as *old* Sapinero was flooded by the reservoir at this spot. U.S. Highway 50 crosses an arm of the reservoir at the Lake Fork of the Gunnison River. Under this water lies the submerged route of track that connected the railroad in the Black Canyon's depths to Lake City (Journey 17). Yes, there was a railroad at the bottom of the Black Canyon—the same railroad, the Denver & Rio Grande, that crested Marshall Pass, served Gunnison, and eventually arrived in Salt Lake City.

Shortly after you pass Blue Mesa's dam, you'll arrive at the Pine Creek trail head. Hike down the trail to take an excellent interpretive boat tour (by reservation) of Morrow Point Reservoir.

Men herded reluctant sheep into narrow-gauge stock cars at Cimarron during brief annual stock rushes (Journey 14). Here the railroad escaped from the Black Canyon via Cimarron Creek and topped Cerro Summit farther west to finally reach Montrose. This route avoided the steepest and narrowest part of the Black Canyon. Don't miss the National Park Service visitors' center at Cimarron or the train displayed on the road to the dam. The track through the Black Canyon was removed in 1948, and its removal finally broke the Narrow Gauge Circle, a route promoted to vacationers that encircled Colorado's spectacular mountains from Salida to Gunnison, Montrose, Ridgway, Telluride, Durango, Chama (New Mexico), Antonito, Alamosa, and back to Salida.

The marina from which the Morrow Point Reservoir boat tours begin is visible in the lower left of this photograph of the reservoir.

The Currecanti Needle was once a symbol of the Denver & Rio Grande Railroad and appeared on their advertising literature. Shown here from the boat tour on Morrow Point Reservoir, the rocky prominence is also visible from the Pioneer Point overlook on Colorado Highway 92.

Locomotive 278 rests on an original bridge at Cimarron, down the short road that leads to the base of Morrow Point Dam. Light enough for the creaky old rails that ran though the Black Canyon and to Crested Butte, it was one of the last two locomotives—the other is in the Gunnison Pioneer Museum—that worked trains on those routes.

Sheep were still being loaded into narrow-gauge trains at Cimarron in September of 1940. *Library of Congress, Russell Lee, LC-USF34-037468-D*

Settlers coveted the waters of the Gunnison River for its irrigation potential. Expeditions down the river in 1900 and 1901 identified this location as the future east portal of the Gunnison Tunnel, a water bore. This tranquil spot along East Portal Road is one of the few places at which automobiles can access the river in the canyon's depths. The road begins inside the southern portion of Black Canyon of the Gunnison National Park.

West of Cimarron, you will climb Cerro Summit and reach the entrance to Black Canyon of the Gunnison National Park. This southern portion of the park is the most popular and includes most of the interpretive facilities. The value of this deepest portion of the canyon was recognized when it became a national monument in March of 1933 and again when it was reclassified as a national park in 1999.

Just a half-dozen miles farther, your journey ends in Montrose. Incorporated shortly before the Denver & Rio Grande railroad reached it in 1882, Montrose became an important commercial center for the region. The Gunnison Tunnel

carried water from the Gunnison River to fields near Montrose, making agriculture a significant factor in its economy. Its historic downtown still bustles with activity. The size of its two-story railroad depot, now the Montrose County Historical Museum (21 North Rio Grande Avenue), confirms the town's economic importance. The Ute Indian Museum and Ouray Memorial Park (17253 Chipeta Road) is just two miles south of town. This museum is located on the homestead that was once the home of Chief Ouray and his wife Chipeta (Journey 15).

The Gunnison River meanders through the Black Canyon of the Gunnison National Park, as seen from the north rim. Though there are few interpretive facilities and access is more difficult (including travel on an unpaved road for part of the route), I prefers the north rim since it is much less crowded, especially in mid-summer.

Cameramen ready themselves to record President William Howard Taft opening the Gunnison Tunnel in 1909. The west portal, shown here, disgorged Gunnison River waters to irrigate farms in the Montrose vicinity.
Library of Congress, Ameron Newman, PAN US GEOG-Colorado No. 1

This view of a small portion of Little Ruin Canyon includes several buildings of the Square Tower Group at Hovenweep National Monument. From left to right are Twin Towers, just below the far canyon rim; Eroded Boulder House, barely visible below the odd-shaped boulder lower in the canyon; Unit Type House in the foreground; and Rim Rock House above the canyon's far rim.

A still-standing wall at Lowry Pueblo includes a door flanked by windows. Pueblo doorways are not very high, perhaps indicating that residents were short in stature.

The Anasazi Heritage Center (27501 Highway 184) is a museum of Ancient Puebloan and other native cultures. There was never an Anasazi tribe; the word is derived from the Navajo term for the peoples that lived here. The center, with two ruins on site, is the perfect introduction to Ancient Puebloan culture. It is also the gateway to Canyons of the Ancients National Monument: 164,000 acres containing about six thousand ruins, mostly unexcavated and undeveloped. Only Lowry Pueblo is developed; it is an interesting stop with forty pueblo rooms, eight kivas, and a Great Kiva.

Hovenweep National Monument, comprised of six villages, straddles the Colorado-Utah border. An 1854 Mormon expedition first reported the existence of ruins here. The Square Tower Group is easily reached via a short walk from the visitors' center. This ancient village surrounds and descends into Little Ruin Canyon. The trail is paved and wheelchair accessible to the first overlook, although steep. An unpaved trail continues to circumnavigate Little Ruin Canyon and is worth the moderately strenuous hike.

Cortez has a historic downtown that includes the Cortez Cultural Center (25 North Market Street) housed in a 1909 commercial building with an unusual painted pressed-metal façade. The Crow Canyon Archaeological Center (23390 Road K) offers hands-on educational programs for all ages. In addition to the

Mesa Verde means "green table," a reference to the trees on the area's plateau tops. Many smaller cliff dwellings dot the canyon walls that separate the mesas in Mesa Verde National Park. The shallow caves provided shelter and perhaps protection against marauders.

Ancient Puebloan culture, the city celebrates other Native American cultures. The Ute Mountain Indian Reservation and the Navajo Indian Reservation are nearby.

Seeking a route from Santa Fe to California, eighteenth-century Spanish explorers named a region of tree-covered plateaus Mesa Verde, or "green table." Prospector John Moss first reported ruins here in 1873. The first white man to enter a Mesa Verde cliff dwelling was photographer W. H. Jackson in 1874. Ranchers soon began to explore (or loot) the ruins. The most extensive early explorations were made by the Wetherill family. Richard Wetherill and Charles Mason are credited with discovering Cliff Palace, Spruce Tree House, and Square Tower House in a single two-day trip in 1889. The four Wetherill brothers claimed to have entered 182 cliff dwellings during 1889 and 1890.

In 1906, Mesa Verde National Park was established as the first national park to preserve the works of people instead of the wonders of nature. The park includes four thousand archaeological sites and six hundred cliff dwellings scattered over almost 82 square miles. Cliff dwellings—pueblos built in the protection of shallow caves—are the feature for which the park is most famous. At Mesa Verde, several cliff dwellings are enormous multistoried villages. Cliff Palace was home to one hundred residents who made use of 150 rooms and 23 kivas. Five of the largest cliff dwellings are accessible by self-guided or ranger-guided tours. Four sites atop the mesas are viewable as self-guided tours. Mesa-top roads provide access to overlooks from which many other cliff dwellings can be viewed. There are three visitors' centers; the first you'll encounter, Far View, also schedules reservations for ranger-guided tours of cliff dwellings.

This 1911 view of Cliff Palace clearly shows the scope of the pueblo. You can imagine the thoughts of the ranchers who stumbled upon these and other similar ruins in the late nineteenth century. Besides rectangular pueblo buildings, a round tower and many kivas are visible. *Library of Congress, LC-USZ62-116571*

GALLOPING GOOSE
Over Lizard Head Pass

Mancos is the starting point for this journey—a journey that will trace the route of the Rio Grande Southern Railroad, which once connected Durango (Journey 15) with Ridgway. The Mancos Valley was settled by white Americans in the 1870s after a large portion of the Ute Mountain Indian Reservation, including the Mancos Valley, was relinquished by the tribe. The town itself was founded in 1894 when the Rio Grande Southern Railroad needed a station here. Mancos was and is an agricultural supply center. Historic buildings line Grand Avenue (south of the main highway), and older residences line side streets. Parts of the downtown resemble an old Western movie set.

Dolores was incorporated in 1900 and served the lumber industry. A tangle of logging railroads spread north from town. To convert those logs into lumber, a sawmill was built at the new town of McPhee, now submerged under the waters of the McPhee Reservoir, visible from the trail at the Anasazi Heritage Center (Journey 13).

Dolores is home to Galloping Goose No. 5. A Galloping Goose is a gasoline-powered railcar, originally built from old automobiles and later from old buses. A single employee would welcome the few passengers aboard, load the mail and possibly some small parcels of freight, and then drive the Goose down the rails—a perfect solution for a remote railroad with little traffic. Goose No. 5 usually rests on rails outside a reconstruction of the Dolores railroad depot, which houses both the Rio Grande Southern Railroad Museum and the Dolores Visitors' Center (421 Railroad Avenue). This small but excellent museum chronicles the history of the railroad and its flock of Geese. Goose No. 5 occasionally flies away, trucked to the narrow-gauge railroads at Durango (Journey 15) or Chama (Journey 16) to again gallop down the rails.

After quite illegally trespassing to explore the San Juan Mountains, white prospectors agitated for the Utes to be removed. The 1873 Brunot Treaty sold four million acres of Ute land in the San Juans, and much more would eventually be taken in the search for riches. Development of southwestern Colorado boomed after that treaty was signed.

Rico is the Spanish word for "rich." Gold was found at the town of Rico during the Civil War, but the discovery of a rich lode of silver in 1879 literally put the town on the map. The Rio Grande Southern's trains reached

DIRECTIONS

Start your journey in Mancos, 28 miles west of Durango. Travel northwest on Colorado Highway 184. Turn right on Colorado Highway 145 to pass through Dolores and Rico to reach the summit of Lizard Head Pass. Near the summit, turn right into the parking lot for the interpretive display about the Rio Grande Southern Railroad.

> **ALTERNATE:** *Continue on Highway 145 if you are averse to unpaved roads. Rejoin the journey at Trout Lake.*

From the parking lot, find unpaved County Road 626 (the old railroad grade). It parallels the paved road northward but then circles around the east side of Trout Lake where there is an old railroad trestle on your left. This road passes a railroad water tank shortly before it rejoins Highway 184 at which you will turn right to reach Ophir.

> **ALTERNATE:** *If you prefer paved roads, continue north on Highway 145 until you reach Colorado Highway Spur 145. Turn right to Telluride.*

Turn left on unpaved County Road 625 at Ophir. If you wish to see the Ames Power plant, turn left on Ames Road. The turn is about ¾-mile from Highway 145 and is not well marked. Return to turn left on County 625. The Illium power plant will be adjacent to the road on your left, followed by a railroad coaling tipple, also on your left but across the river. When you reach Colorado Highway 145, turn right and then follow Spur 145 to Telluride.

From Telluride, drive west on Spur 145. At the junction with Highway 145, continue westward until you reach Placerville. Turn right on Colorado Highway 62, which will take you over Dallas Divide into Ridgway, the end of your journey.

This studio portrait was taken after the signing of the Brunot Treaty in 1873. Otto Mears is in the middle row at far right. In the front row from left to right is Guerro (Ouray's father), Chipeta (Ouray's wife), Chief Ouray, and Piah (Tabeguache Ute Chief). *Denver Public Library, Western History Collection, William Gunnison Chamberlain, X-19251*

Rico in 1891. In 1892, the railroad built a mountainous branch to the mines east of town, Rico's population reached five thousand, and the usual mining town diversions—twenty-three saloons and a red-light district—took root. Nevertheless, a bank, churches, a theater, a boarding house, and the railroad seemed to assure future prosperity. Then came repeal of the Sherman Silver Purchase Act in 1893. The town's economy vanished almost overnight. Trains no longer rumbled from the mines with loads of silver; the track was even removed. By 1900, only eight hundred stubborn souls clung to a rugged, isolated existence in Rico. Mining recovered in the 1920s and eventually shifted its focus from silver to lead and zinc.

Downtown Rico displays many historic structures, including a wonderful stone courthouse. The railroad yard was west of the highway; its most significant remnant is the water tank that filled the tenders of thirsty steam locomotives about to climb Lizard Head Pass. You can't miss the surface plants of some of the historic mines that are just north of town.

The Rio Grande Southern crested the 10,222-foot Lizard Head Pass, where today you can examine a display about the railroad's history. It maintained a wye (a track for turning locomotives and snowplows) here as well as stock pens. Every fall, huge trains of sheep—some requiring four locomotives—were loaded here and at other stations onto double-decked, narrow-gauge stock cars for a trip to lower winter ranges or for a final trip to the stockyards. These stock rushes occurred all over Colorado but were especially spectacular on the Rio Grande Southern, a railroad that slumbered most of the year with very few steam trains and an occasional Galloping Goose. The last stock rush on the Rio Grande Southern occurred in 1949, when a *half million* sheep were moved by just this one railroad. Its trains hauled thousands of cars full of the wooly creatures behind every antique steam locomotive that could be made to move!

Lizard Head Pass was named for the rock formation visible above this Rio Grande Southern passenger train. The odd-shaped peak is west of the modern highway. Tiny locomotive No. 9 pulls a single car named for the mining town of Rico. This train is likely a photographer's special, with the passenger car containing the chemical lab needed to prepare and develop glass-plate negatives. *Denver Public Library, Western History Collection, William Henry Jackson, WHJ-446*

An unpaved road, the railroad's old grade north of Lizard Head Pass, can be used to circle Trout Lake, where you can glimpse an old railroad trestle at the far end of the lake and a railroad water tank close to where the unpaved road rejoins the main highway

The mining town of Ophir, named after the biblical location of King Solomon's mines, was the western end of the Ophir Loop, a special section of railroad track. Trains dropped down the mountainside from Trout Lake, circled back at Ophir, and rolled down the valley of the South Fork of the San Miguel River just below the upper track.

Your journey continues on an unpaved road from Ophir down the San Miguel River valley. A more minor road leads to the Ames power plant. Ames was the location of the world's first commercial alternating-current power plant. By the spring of 1891, the plant was supplying current to run the pumps that drained the Gold

The passengers of northbound Rio Grande Southern trains gasped at this view of the San Miguel River valley as they started down the Ophir Loop. After circling to the right, their train would travel down the valley to the junction with the Telluride branch. This is the identical view from your automobile on Colorado Highway 145.

King Mine, 3.5 miles distant. Thomas Edison championed direct current, which could not be sent long distances. Nikola Tesla and the Westinghouse Electric Company promoted alternating current which, though unproven, was purported to be able to reach the mine. The mine's owners had no choice but to gamble on alternating current. The mines were flooding, and no other source of energy was a viable option. This hydroelectric plant's turbines are spun by water from Trout Lake. A newer plant replaced the original and still operates today.

Back on the road down the San Miguel River, you'll pass a stone building at Illium, another power plant that reused the water from the Ames plant to generate more electricity. Farther along and across the river, you can see a large timber structure that was used to store and load coal into railroad tenders near Vance Junction, where a branch line track diverged to serve Telluride.

Remote Telluride was a showplace mining town with the same amenities as Aspen, Cripple Creek, or Leadville. Founded in 1878 as Columbia, its name was changed to Telluride in 1887. Gold was first discovered here in 1858, but development was slow because of its remote location until the Rio Grande Southern Railroad arrived in 1890. The infamous Butch Cassidy's first major crime was robbing Telluride's San Miguel Valley Bank in 1889. All of Telluride's historic mines—including the Pandora, Sheridan, Smuggler-Union, and Tomboy—were eventually consolidated into the Idarado Mining Company (now part of Newmont Mining). Their extensive network of tunnels underlies virtually the entire area between Telluride and Silverton. An Idarado mine surface plant is on the Million Dollar Highway between Silverton and Ouray (Journey 15).

During World War II, worthless uranium ore that had been accumulating in the waste dumps of mines was hauled away by narrow-gauge steam trains for refinement into fuel for the world's first atomic weapons. Armed federal agents rode the antique steam trains to protect their cargo.

The first ski lift was installed in Telluride in 1972, and skiing slowly replaced mining as the town's major industry. As the final ore was being trundled out of the Pandora Mine, tourism became a year-around business, with summer activities augmenting skiing. There are still many historic structures in Telluride, including the legendary New Sheridan Hotel (231 West Colorado Avenue). The Telluride Historical Museum (201 West Gregory Avenue) is housed in the historic Miner's Hospital building.

The Rio Grande Southern's shops were in the railroad town of Ridgway, incorporated in 1891. That year, tourists started traveling by train to the summit

TELLURIDE-LIZARD HEAD AREA

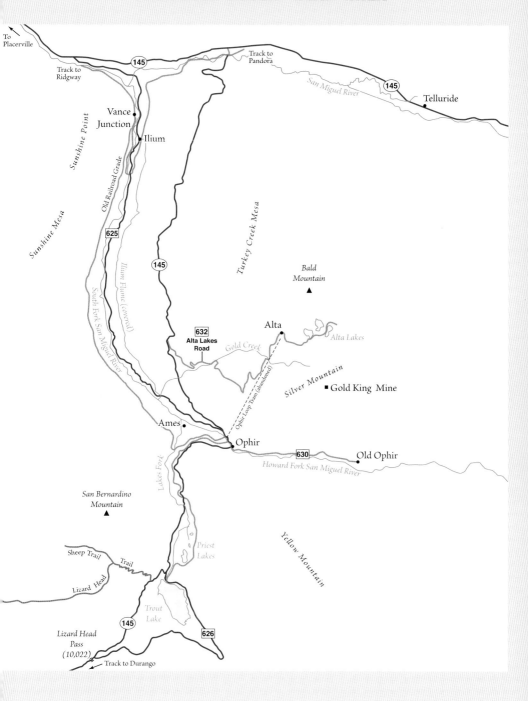

of Pikes Peak as luxury hotels and fine restaurants catered to wealthy visitors up and down Colorado's eastern mountains. In contrast, southwestern Colorado was still remote and rugged. Otto Mears's construction of the Rio Grande Southern Railroad was about to open up this isolated land. Mears had built the Silverton Railroad, but it fell short of reaching Ouray by a rugged 8 miles (Journey 15). To bridge this tiny gap, he built 162 miles of the Rio Grande Southern! A train journey from Silverton to Ouray started on the Denver & Rio Grande branch line from Silverton to Durango and ended on another Denver & Rio Grande branch line from Ridgway to Ouray. You can only wonder how many people chose the 235-mile train trip instead of the 8-mile bone-breaking jaunt in a stagecoach.

The Rio Grande Southern served mines, logging stands, small towns, and ranches, but it never generated much traffic. All of its almost fifty locomotives were purchased secondhand. It couldn't even pay its operating expenses, let alone return the investor's capitol that built the spectacular line. It survived only sixty years, a short lifespan for a railroad. Ridgway's depot still stands, and the Ridgway Railroad Museum (150 Racecourse Road) will interpret the railroad's history for you, but the museum's main attraction is an accurate, full-size working replica of Goose No. 1.

The view of the mountain barrier westward from Telluride's Main Street vividly demonstrates why this portion of Colorado was wild and remote long after much of the region became settled and even urbane. When this photo was exposed in 1908, Telluride's substantial buildings included the New Sheridan Hotel, the Daily Journal, the tower-like First National Bank, and numerous retail establishments. Wagon roads—now four-wheel-drive adventures—traversed the mountains to Silverton and Ouray. One, the Black Bear Road, was even the inspiration for a song recorded by entertainer C. W. McCall.
Colorado Historical Society, Joseph E. Byers, CHS.X4755

OTTO MEARS, a Russian immigrant, served in the Civil War and later headed west to find his fortune. In 1871, Mears started to construct a network of toll roads through Colorado's mountains. Mears' roads were gradually replaced by railroads, a trend that was not lost upon him. In 1882 and 1883, Mears built a toll road between Silverton and Ouray, tapping the Red Mountain Mining District. It was here that Mears decided to launch his first railroad venture. The Silverton Railroad (Journey 15) connected Silverton with the Red Mountain Mining District; its trains struggled to 11,113 feet above the sea to do so.

Promoter Mears attracted attention by adding elegant dining service and a sleeping car on a railroad only eighteen miles long. The industry practice at the time was that railroad passes—small printed cards—were issued by the railroads to anyone and everyone who might benefit the line. Mears did his competitors one better by printing Silverton Railroad passes on buckskin. Some were crafted from filigreed silver and a few from gold.

Mears would eventually purchase two more railroads connecting Silverton to other mining districts, giving him a 40-mile railroad empire high in the Colorado mountains. He then built the 162-mile Rio Grande Southern Railroad (Journey 14) between Durango and Ridgway, which became a rolling relic that spent many of its years in bankruptcy and never paid the cost of construction back to its investors, let alone a profit!

Otto Mears' ashes were scattered over the San Juan Mountains after his 1931 death. The little railroads out of Silverton lay dormant, with the last rails removed in 1942 to be melted and reused as armaments in World War II. The Rio Grande Southern expired in 1951. Had it survived another decade, it might have become the premier tourist railroad in Colorado—so spectacular was the scenery—but in 1951, southwestern Colorado was too remote to attract many tourists.

Otto Mears' first railroad, the Silverton Railroad, served the town of Red Mountain. The depot at bottom right is surrounded by a "wye" track, which allowed the little trains to reverse direction. The wye track was necessary because the town was on a stub of track and trains needed to travel back the way they came. The large building on the left, the National Belle Mine, still stands. *Denver Public Library, Western History Collection, X-61973*

LOST SOULS
Through the San Juan Mountains

Ouray was incorporated in 1876, the hundredth year of the existence of the United States. Prospectors arrived here a year earlier. In 1887, the Denver & Rio Grande built a narrow-gauge track from Montrose to Ouray, but steep, rocky walls made railroad construction from Ouray virtually impossible in every other compass direction. Ironton's ore, which had been hauled down the difficult toll road to Ouray, found the route to Silverton an easy trip on the new Silverton Railroad, which was completed in 1889.

Driving today's paved highways, it is difficult to understand that Telluride, Ouray, Silverton, and Lake City were all really part of the same mineral-rich locale. You have to escape to steep, rocky tracks—the province of four-wheel-drive vehicles and mountain goats—to see how close these towns are to each other.

Tourists arrived in the area in 1888, and soon the Denver & Rio Grande Railroad was promoting the Narrow Gauge Circle excursion. Starting and ending in Salida, you parallel most of it on Journeys 11, 12, 15, and 16. Since the section between Ouray and Ironton was a rough stagecoach ride, the tourist route switched there to the Rio Grande Southern Railroad (Journey 14) after 1891.

Like Georgetown, Ouray never experienced a devastating fire, so many of its nineteenth-century buildings still stand; a walk around town is a must. St. Joseph's Miners' Hospital opened its doors in 1887, and its building now hosts the Ouray County Museum (420 Sixth Avenue). You can experience underground mining at the Bachelor-Syracuse Mine (1222 County Road 14).

In 1883, Otto Mears built a toll road between Ouray and Ironton. It would eventually be called the Million Dollar Highway, for the modern, paved highway supposedly cost millions of dollars per mile to construct between Ouray and the summit of Red Mountain Pass. Another story is that the fill material used to build the highway was actually ore containing millions of dollars of gold. The truth is lost along with the other barroom conversations of 1920s Silverton.

Climbing the Million Dollar Highway, you'll pass the surface plant of the Idarado Mine on your left. Just past the mine, turn right into a well-marked overlook with an exceptional view of, and great interpretive exhibits about, the Red Mountain Mining District. You'll be amazed at the panoramic scope of the district and the seemingly impossible route of the Silverton Railway. Think about how much wealth must have created this huge industrial area, much of

DIRECTIONS

Start at Ouray on U.S. Highway 550, south of Montrose. The Bachelor Syracuse mine tour is just north of Ouray and then east on County Road 14. From Ouray, drive south on U.S. 550—this is the famous Million Dollar Highway—to Silverton. Be sure to stop at the Red Mountain Mining District interpretive overlook on your right. At Silverton, turn left on Greene Street, the town's main street. Turn right on County Road 2, just past the courthouse and museum. You'll discover an interpretive overlook on your right and then the Mayflower Mill on your left.

> **OPTIONAL:** *After the mill, you will lose pavement. At Howardsville, you can turn right on County Road 4 and then travel on County Road 4A for the Old Hundred Gold Mine Tour. Retrace your steps and continue on County 2 to Eureka. The road begins to climb here where it is located atop the old Silverton Northern Railroad grade for the last 4 miles to Animas Forks.*

Retrace your route to Silverton. Follow U.S. 550 south to Durango, where it joins U.S. Highway 160. Follow U.S. 160 east and turn right on Colorado Highway 172 to reach Ignacio. Turn left on Colorado Highway 151 in Ignacio. In Arboles, you can follow County Road 982, marked Navajo State Park, to the right to reach the railroad display, which will be on your left on the Windsurf Beach road. Return to Highway 151 and turn right.

> **ALTERNATE:** *If you prefer pavement or wish to see the Chimney Rock Archaeological Site (by reservation), continue on Highway 151. Chimney Rock is a left turn. Return to Highway 151 and turn left. Turn right on U.S. 160. End your journey in Pagosa Springs.*

North of Arboles, turn right on unpaved County Road 500/F. After passing through Pagosa Junction, continue north on County Road 17.50/700 to reach a small portion of County Road Q, which will take you to U.S. 160. Turn right on U.S. 160 to reach Pagosa Springs and the end of your journey.

This tunnel on Otto Mears' toll road, south of Ouray, is cut not through rock but through snow. In August of 1882, this stagecoach had to burrow under an avalanche that had buried the road in the winter of 1881! Note the broken trees and other avalanche debris. This section of the Million Dollar Highway still suffers avalanches, and a monument along the road honors snowplow drivers who have lost their lives keeping Colorado's highways open. *Library of Congress, LC-USF344-007609-ZB*

which is over 11,000 feet high and covered in feet of winter snow. Remember that this is just *one* of several mining districts from Telluride through Silverton to Lake City!

Not far south of the overlook, there is an unpaved road that leads east to the site of Red Mountain Town. Though the road may not be suitable for ordinary passenger vehicles, it is a short walk into the town site. A large structure of the National Belle Mine still stands here.

Silverton was connected to the outside world by railroad in 1882. Its population peaked at around five thousand souls. Those nineteenth-century mountain pioneers dined at restaurants in the remote San Juan Mountains that served fine wines with lobster. The wealth that gave birth to elegance in this remote land was tapped by four railroads that moved ore to and from three smelters and thirty mills.

The site of Red Mountain Town, pictured on page 143, still shelters one building of the National Belle mine. The piles of rock behind the building are waste from the mine, called tailings.

Silverton has also seen rough times. The Silver Panic arrived in 1893; the 1918 flu epidemic decimated the already-dwindling population; metal prices fell; a mountain lake collapsed into a mine; and the last major mine closed in 1991. After World War II, however, both Hollywood and tourists discovered Silverton. Movies were filmed here and, in quite a surprise to the railroad, the Denver & Rio Grande's narrow-gauge, steam-powered trains from Durango began to carry passengers again—lots of passengers.

That railroad, now the Durango & Silverton Narrow Gauge Railroad, operates the Freight Yard Museum (10th and Animas streets) in the old Silverton depot. Here, you'll see a model of the Silverton Railway's Corkscrew Turntable and learn about its heart-stopping operations. The location of the original turntable is illustrated in the interpretive exhibit at the overlook near the Idarado Mine. You can see, or even stay at, the Grand Imperial Hotel (1219 Greene

Street), built in 1883, and visit the San Juan County Historical Society Museum (15th and Greene streets).

If you crave adventure but are not too adventurous, follow the Animas River northeast out of Silverton. The grade of the Silverton Northern Railroad also follows the river near this mostly unpaved road. Stop at the overlook and

SILVERTON AREA

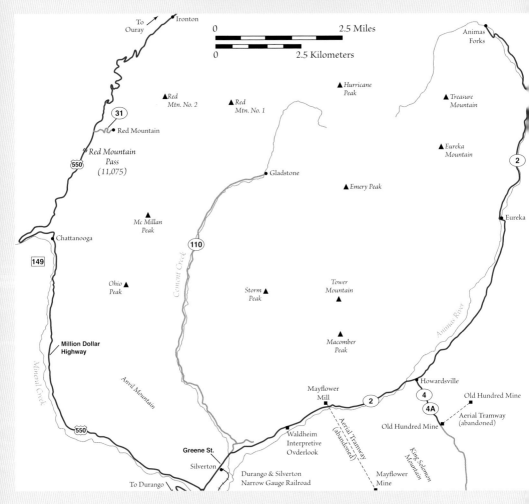

Silverton lies in Bakers Park, a small, flat valley whose floor is 9,318 feet above the sea. Storm Peak, rising in the background to 13,487 feet, is just one of many "thirteeners" that surround the town.

interpretive exhibit at the site of the Silver Lake Mill. The Waldheim mansion once stood on the riverbank below you, as did the huge Silver Lake Mill. In the distance, you'll see the Mayflower Mill, which will be your next stop.

The Mayflower was the last mill to close in the district—it ceased operations along with the Sunnyside Mine in 1991. Unlike most historic mills, the Mayflower was left intact. It was built in the 1930s, when its machinery was moved into place via the now-gone Silverton Northern Railroad. With the railroad gone and old machinery not in demand, it was deemed best to donate the intact industrial plant to the San Juan County Historical Society. The Mayflower is consequently the most complete historic mill left in Colorado. A self-guided tour will let you explore as many or as few details as you wish—and there is much to explore. Don't miss the cable tramway that carries ore buckets (still hanging on the cable) from the mine high on the mountainside across from the mill. Bring your binoculars or a long telephoto lens on your camera to glimpse the tramway's distant eastern terminus.

Locomotive Eureka meditates before her morning run south from Silverton. This antique wood-burning locomotive is a guest here, having traveled from Nevada to take part in a yearly celebration named Railfest. The regular locomotives of the Durango & Silverton Narrow Gauge Railroad are much larger and burn coal.

The mill at Eureka is gone, but its foundations are clearly visible on the mountainside in the lower left corner of this photograph. Mills were constructed on hillsides so that gravity would move the ore from one step of the milling process to the next. The concentrated minerals were loaded into railroad cars at the bottom of the structure.

Turn right at Howardsville to tour the Old Hundred Gold Mine. Back on the main road, continue until you reach the town site of Eureka. The large timber structure here was once the railroad's water tank. Little is left of the mill at Eureka, but its foundations are clearly visible on the mountainside. Your road crosses over to the south side of the river and becomes the old railroad grade. These last 4 miles of the railroad were the first to be abandoned. Otto Mears had extended his railroad to Animas Forks so that the mines, mills, and railroad could operate year round, but the first winter saw the railroad closed by hundreds of inches of snow. Mears prepared for the next winter by enclosing most of those 4 miles of track in timber snow sheds. Imagine the sinking feeling—shared by Mears, the mine owners, and the 450 Animas Forks residents—when the first avalanche of the season wiped out Mears' investment in those structures!

Drive those last four miles to Animas Forks, where a surprising number of buildings stand, the oldest of which was built in 1873. There is a walking-tour brochure of this ghost town, which is highly recommended. Before the railroad arrived in 1904, the town was supplied from Lake City via the Cinnamon Pass Road, today suitable only for four-wheel-drive vehicles.

The Denver & Rio Grande Railroad founded Durango in 1880 as a home for its roundhouse and other facilities. Ignoring the existing hamlet of Hermosa, the railroad made money by building Durango and reaping the profits from increased land values due to the railroad's very presence. Though the Denver &

Passengers made their tedious narrow-gauge way over mountain passes to remote Durango to be greeted by the most modern transportation convenience: an electric trolley car. *Colorado Historical Society, CHS.X6814*

CHIEF OURAY WAS BORN IN TAOS, New Mexico, in 1833 of an Uncompahgre Ute mother and a half Jicarilla Apache father. At Taos, he not only learned to speak the local language of Spanish but also English. Only later did he learn Apache and Ute. Ouray, who became chief at age seventeen, led the Utes in a time of great upheaval as their lands were relentlessly pilfered by whites. He understood that negotiating a settlement with the U.S. government was the only hope for his people against a formidable foe. Influenced by his wife, Chipeta, he negotiated treaties that supposedly ended hostilities and settled the Utes on reservations.

Little by little, white Americans chipped away at the reservation lands, and the Utes were rightfully incensed. Congress introduced a bill in 1878 calling for the removal of the Utes from all of Colorado. The Meeker Massacre (Journey 3) occurred in 1879. In the end, little could be done. The lands were gone. Otto Mears, Indian agent at the time, negotiated a treaty in 1880 that confined the Utes to the three reservations they now occupy, two in Colorado and one in Utah. He paid each Ute male who would sign the treaty the sum of two dollars.

Chipeta was born Kiowa Apache in 1844 and married Ouray in 1859. Present at many treaty negotiations, she had a strong influence on Ouray, and she even traveled to Washington, D.C., with him. She died in 1924.

Ouray and Chipeta homesteaded eight acres near Montrose, and it is here that Chipeta is buried. The site now hosts the Ute Indian Museum and Ouray Memorial Park (Journey 12). Ouray died in 1880 and is buried at Ignacio.

Chief Ouray and his wife, Chipeta, pose for a formal portrait. *Denver Public Library, Western History Collection, Walker Art Studio, X-30600*

Rio Grande is gone, the trains to Silverton are now operated by the Durango & Silverton Narrow Gauge Railroad. The railroad operates from the original depot (479 Main Avenue), and half of their roundhouse is now a superb museum. Downtown offers both original historic buildings, including the 1887 Strater Hotel (699 Main Avenue), and new buildings constructed in the style of the old. Tour the Animas Museum (3065 West 2nd Avenue).

Durango's Fort Lewis College began as an Indian school, established in 1891 after the U.S. Army's fort was deactivated. It was located 16 miles southwest of Durango on the Ute Mountain Indian Reservation and moved to its present location on a mesa overlooking Durango in 1956.

The Ute Indians inhabited the mountains of Colorado, as well as nearby areas of Utah and New Mexico, after the Ancient Puebloans departed (Journey 13). Both white settlers and miners coveted their lands, and treaties gradually reduced the Ute's presence to the Ute Mountain and Southern Ute Reservations in Colorado and the Uintah and Ouray Indian Reservation in Utah. Ignacio is the headquarters of the present-day Southern Ute tribe. Ignacio's Southern Ute Indian Cultural Center Museum (14826 Highway 172) is a professionally executed interpretive museum accented with many beautiful artifacts. As the time of this book's writing, the tribe is building a larger museum, also in Ignacio.

Narrow-gauge freight trains still ran from Chama to Durango though Arboles as late as 1968. You'll find a water tank as well as two railroad cars resting on a short section of track near Navajo Lake at Arboles. The display is off the main road. At Arboles, you have a choice of routes.

If pavement and pueblo history appeal to you, continue north toward Chimney Rock. The Chimney Rock Archaeological Area is a small but spectacularly beautiful Ancestral Puebloan site. Access is only by guided two-and-a-half-hour walking tours that occur just a few times a day, so plan ahead.

If your tastes run to unpaved byways and railroad history, continue west from Arboles along the San Juan River to Pagosa Junction (also known as Gato). Here you'll find a railroad water tank, a substantial railroad bridge, railroad cars, narrow-gauge track still on the ground, and other railroad-related structures. These artifacts were also part of the line connecting Chama with Durango. They're located on the Jicarilla Apache Indian Reservation, so please respect this private property.

Either route will end at Pagosa Springs, the 1878 site of Fort Lewis. Mineral-laden hot springs had attracted people for centuries, but the town of Pagosa

Springs was not incorporated until 1891. The word Pagosa is derived from Navaho words that translate as "bad-smelling water." Original ownership of the hot springs was disputed between the Navaho and Ute tribes. This was unusual in Colorado since communal use, such as that in Manitou Springs, was the more common practice. Indian claims made little difference when, in 1880, the U.S. government took the springs as its own, and the town of Pagosa Springs began to grow. The Rio Grande, Pagosa & Northern Railroad whistled into Pagosa Springs in 1900. This connecting railroad—eventually part of the Denver & Rio Grande—provided a commercial outlet for the town via Pagosa Junction. Logging became an important industry once railroads were available to transport logs to the mill and lumber from the mill to distant markets. Take the walking tour of old downtown Pagosa Springs and visit the San Juan Historical Society Museum (96 Pagosa Street, Highway 160).

Pagosa Springs was but a shadow of its current self when this photo was exposed, probably between 1890 and 1895. The notation on the photo incorrectly reads "Largest Hot Spring in the World." A few commercial buildings stand in the background exactly where the old downtown exists today. *Colorado Historical Society, D. C. Desmond, CHS.X4615*

SOUTH CENTRAL COLORADO
Hispanic Heritage

SPANISH EXPLORERS ARRIVED in the region that is now south central Colorado in the sixteenth century. Many Hispanic families in the San Luis Valley and along the southern Front Range trace their origins to Spain, not to Mexico. Even more so than southwestern Colorado (Chapter 4), this region has retained its historic character. Spanish explorers, Italian coal miners, Native Americans, Mormon farmers, and English railroad builders all crossed paths here. It is a most interesting region of Colorado.

Festive musicians prepare to perform in front of Walsenburg's Sporleder Hotel in 1882. *Denver Public Library, Western History Collection, X-15097*

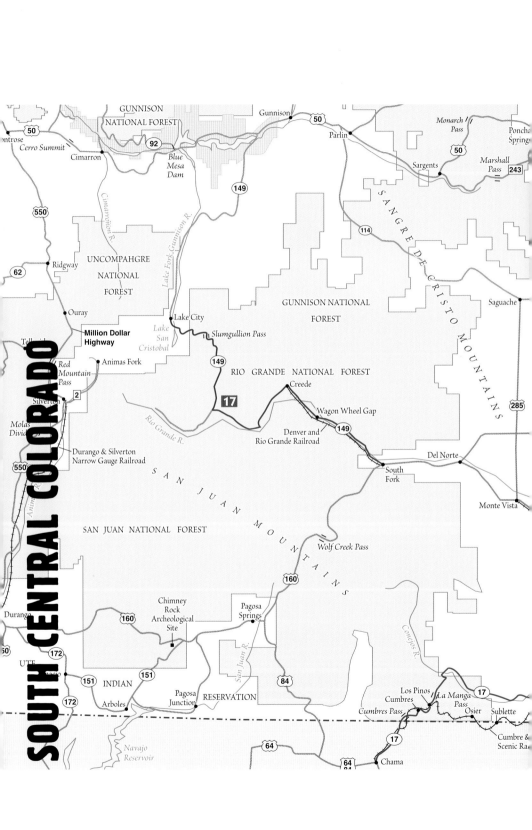

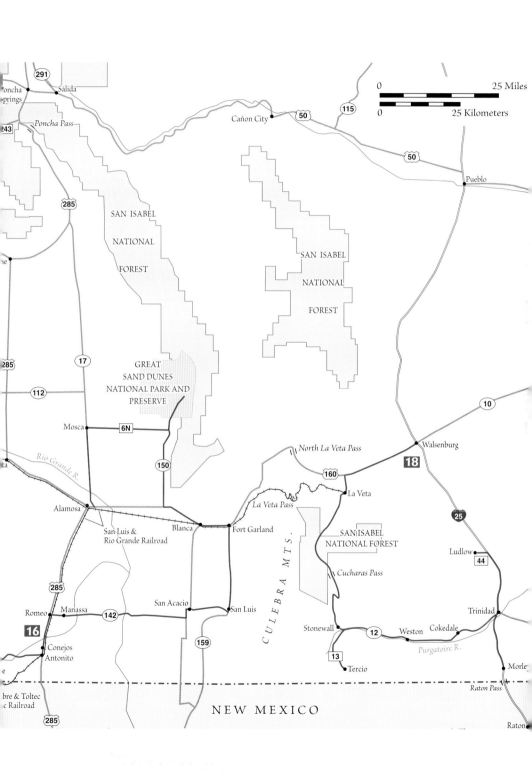

EXPLORERS
Into the San Luis Valley

The first European settlement near what is now Chama, New Mexico, was San Juan de los Caballeros, founded in 1598. This area would eventually become part of the United States, and other ethnic groups would join the Spaniards and Native Americans already living in the region. The narrow-gauge rails of the Denver & Rio Grande reached Chama on the last day of 1880. More than most western towns, small and remote Chama maintains its historic ambiance.

THE DENVER & RIO GRANDE RAILROAD

GENERAL WILLIAM JACKSON PALMER chose to build a narrow-gauge railroad from Denver to Mexico City starting in 1870. It would never reach Mexico City, but it would cover Colorado's mountains with a web of rails, both narrow and standard gauge. A narrow-gauge mainline would reach west to Salt Lake City, Utah, and was later replaced by a standard-gauge connection. The Rio Grande would merge with the Moffat railroad, and its trains burrowed through the mountains in the six-mile-long Moffat Tunnel. Today, the "Grande" is part of the Union Pacific. Some of its tracks became independent short-line railroads. Over 100 miles of its 1,800-mile narrow-gauge empire are still operated as preserved railways.

The Denver & Rio Grande was a unique combination of modern standard-gauge and antique narrow-gauge railroading. One of the railroad's more modern 1923 steam locomotives simmers quietly on narrow-gauge rails, while an early standard-gauge diesel locomotive growls softly at the extensive Alamosa shops in 1958. *Denver Public Library, Western History Collection, Otto C. Perry, OP-7630*

DIRECTIONS

Start your journey at the railroad yard in Chama, New Mexico, southeast of Pagosa Springs. Follow New Mexico Highway 17 northeast toward Cumbres Pass. The road becomes Colorado Highway 17 at the border. After exploring the railroad facilities at Cumbres Pass, continue on Highway 17 to Antonito. Follow U.S. Highway 285 north from Antonito. Turn right on Colorado Highway 142 at Romeo to pass through Manassa and reach San Luis. In San Luis, turn left on Colorado Highway 159 to reach Fort Garland, where you will turn left on U.S. Highway 160. Turn right on Colorado Highway 150 to reach the Great Sand Dunes National Park and Preserve. You'll leave the park on the same road but will shortly turn right on County Road 6N to reach Mosca. Turn left on Colorado Highway 17 at Mosca. Turn right on U.S. 160 to end your journey in Alamosa.

It may seem odd that the best-preserved "Colorado" railroad town is actually in New Mexico, but that is the case. The railroad constructed substantial facilities at Chama, a helper station where additional locomotives were added to eastbound trains about to climb the steep grade over Cumbres Pass. Even with those extra locomotives, some trains had to be moved uphill in several pieces and then reassembled at the summit. Locomotives and cars had to be serviced and fresh train crews supplied. These activities required a large railroad yard with all the facilities of nineteenth-century railroading. Remarkably, almost all of the original facilities are still here, and you can still ride over Cumbres Pass on the Cumbres & Toltec Scenic Railroad.

This train of the Cumbres & Toltec Scenic Railroad just departed from Osier and is climbing Cumbres Pass before beginning its steep descent into Chama. Osier's several restored historic structures include this original water tank, which is still used by steam locomotives.

The last steam-powered freight train whistled through town in 1968 on its way from Durango to Alamosa. By then, it was evident that the railroad at Chama was historically significant and must be saved. Sixty-four miles of mainline track from Chama to Antonito were preserved along with all the railroad facilities along the way. A support group, the Friends of the Cumbres & Toltec Scenic Railroad, not only restores the many historical artifacts on the railroad but also interprets its history for visitors. This organization publishes superb walking-tour brochures for the Chama, Cumbres Pass, and Antonito railroad yards. Walk around the railroad yard at Chama and ride the train from either Chama or Antonito.

Antonito and the adjacent town of Conejos are near the southern end of the San Luis Valley. This incredible 7,000-foot, mountain-rimmed valley is about the size of the state of Connecticut. Antonito is now the eastern terminus of the Cumbres & Toltec Scenic Railroad, but once the tracks from Alamosa diverged here. Rails headed west to Chama, Durango, and Silverton, and a long-gone branch routed trains south to Santa Fe, New Mexico. The latter branch, removed in 1941, was nicknamed the Chili Line for the colorful ristras of chili peppers hung on homes along the way. The depot used by the preserved railroad is not a historic structure, but the original stone depot built by the Denver & Rio Grande still stands in Antonito, as do other historic buildings.

Conejos is home to the oldest Catholic parish in Colorado, Our Lady of Guadalupe (6633 County Road 13), established in 1858. A second church building was finished by 1863. That building was destroyed by fire in 1926 and the current church built to replace it. There are several contestants for the title of "oldest church in Colorado." The details of the argument are less important than the beautiful old church buildings at Conejos, Viejo San Acacio, and San Luis.

Manassa—founded by Mormon settlers in 1878—was the birthplace of legendary boxer Jack Dempsey, nicknamed the Manassa Mauler. The cabin in which he was born is now the small Jack Dempsey Museum and Park (412 Main Street), honoring the man who was heavyweight champion from 1919 to 1926.

A major historic artifact in San Acacio is the two-story depot of the vanished San Luis Valley Southern Railroad. The structure is now a bed-and-breakfast but was built to accommodate passengers and freight on this short, 32-mile railroad from Blanca to the New Mexico border. The depot building, north of the highway, was also the railroad's headquarters until 1950. Its trains were part of a plan promoted by the Costilla Estates Development Company to develop towns and farms along its route. The Catholic church building at Viejo (Old) San Acacio was built in 1856.

San Luis, established in 1851, is the oldest town in Colorado. The San Luis Museum and Cultural Center (401 Church Place) is located here, as are many historic structures. The first Sangre de Cristo Parish church building (511 Church Place) was constructed at San Luis in 1854, but the current building dates from later in the nineteenth century, when the area was served by French priests. Water is a critical resource in the American West, and the oldest water district in Colorado is located here—its claim on the liquid gold dates to an irrigation ditch completed in 1852. A trail rises to the Shrine of the Stations of the Cross above town and offers a panorama of the San Luis Valley in addition to religious inspiration.

The Sangre de Cristo church in San Luis was built in the last part of the nineteenth century. Its architecture is a unique combination of adobe and stylistic elements influenced by the French clergy who manned the parish during this period.

After the San Luis Valley became part of the United States, the U.S. government built Fort Massachusetts in 1852 to protect settlers from Indians. Its location proved unsuitable, and in 1858, Fort Garland was built six miles farther south. Its troops defeated a Confederate force in the Civil War battle of New Mexico's Glorieta Pass. The fort's most famous commander was the celebrated frontiersman Kit Carson, who commanded volunteers here starting in 1866 in the absence of regular army troops. Those regular troops returned the following year, and Carson then moved to Boggsville (Journey 19), where he died in 1868. The famous Buffalo Soldiers, African-American soldiers, served here from 1876 to 1879. After the Utes were moved to reservations, Fort Garland's usefulness ended, and it was abandoned in 1883. It is now the Fort Garland Museum (29477 Highway 159).

Soldiers still manned Fort Garland when this remarkable photo was taken in 1874. Today, the fort is a museum operated by the Colorado Historical Society. *Library of Congress, Timothy H. O'Sullivan, LC-DIG-stereo-1s00371*

About 30 square miles of sand dunes rise 750 feet from the San Luis Valley's floor. In 1932, those 30 square miles became part of the Great Sand Dunes National Monument. In 2004, the momument was expanded into the Great Sand Dunes National Park and Preserve, quadruple its original size. Portions of the Sangre de Cristo Mountains bordering the eastern edge of the dunes are included in the national park, so hiking includes forested slopes and alpine lakes. The increased size helped protect the water necessary for the dunes to exist. Both wind and water created and continue to expand the dunes. Currently, Great Sand Dunes National Park and Preserve encompass about 150,000 acres, with a high point over 13,000 feet. Ulysses Herard homesteaded along Medano Creek in 1875. That creek is now in the park and enthralls visitors with its unusual and frequent periodic surges of water.

The Great Sand Dunes National Park and Preserve contains many square miles of dunes, as well as mountain peaks exceeding 13,000 feet.

The Denver & Rio Grande built track over La Veta Pass into the San Luis Valley. The railroad chose a bend in the Rio Grande River as a location for its shops and named it Alamosa—Spanish for "cottonwood." In June of 1878, one of the first trains to arrive was laden with buildings from the construction camp of Garland City, which were promptly unloaded onto the new town's lots. Instant Alamosa! The railroad's shops provided employment for several hundred people as rails—some standard gauge and some narrow gauge—radiated from Alamosa in every direction.

This view of the mountains surrounding the San Luis Valley greeted passengers as they dropped down the west side of La Veta Pass. In the earliest days, the valley's central city of Alamosa was just a stop on the way to mining camps at Silverton or Creede.

An 1891 fire wiped Alamosa's old hand-me-down buildings off the map. Alamosa grew into a city with churches, schools, and banks replacing saloons, "houses of ill repute," and gambling dens. As mining declined in importance, so did the railroad lines that served mining towns. Slowly, the town became a center for agriculture. The San Luis Valley's economy is still strongly agricultural, and

Alamosa's large brick depot was constructed after a 1907 fire destroyed the original structure. Its size speaks to the importance of Alamosa as a railroad center.

trainloads of barley for making Coors beer are hauled over La Veta Pass. In 1925, the first students were enrolled at Alamosa's Adams State Normal School, which evolved into today's Adams State College.

Narrow-gauge cars of crude oil arrived at Alamosa's refinery from the oil-loading racks at Chama. After World War II, drilling pipe was shipped from Alamosa to Farmington, New Mexico, on the longest trains the antique narrow-gauge railroad had ever seen. Today, Alamosa is the commercial center of the San Luis Valley. Walk around the old business district on the east end of town and don't miss the San Luis Valley Museum (306 Hunt Avenue, behind the visitors' center) or the large 1907 Denver & Rio Grande depot (610 State Avenue). The vast dual-gauge railroad yards and shops vanished in the early 1970s. The San Luis & Rio Grande Railroad replaced the Denver & Rio Grande, and Rio Grande Scenic Railroad (601 State Avenue) passenger trains still depart Alamosa for the crossing of La Veta Pass. Some trains even travel to Antonito to connect with the Cumbres & Toltec Scenic Railroad.

NO NIGHT
Over Slumgullion Pass

South Fork was a stage stop for those traveling to Lake City over Slumgullion Pass. South Fork's economy relied on ranching, farming, and logging. Sawmills were constructed, and the railroad carried lumber to market. The only remaining Denver & Rio Grande water tank built to serve standard-gauge steam locomotives can be seen on the north side of Highway 160.

DIRECTIONS

South Fork is west of Alamosa on U.S. Highway 160. Take the road to the right, Colorado Highway 149, through Wagon Wheel Gap to Creede.

OPTIONAL: *The unpaved Bachelor Loop includes the ghost town of Bachelor and many old mines. You should purchase an inexpensive guidebook for this tour from the Creede Chamber of Commerce. For an abbreviated tour of the mines, drive north from Creede on Forest Road 503. You will pass many mines, some near the road and some on top of the towering cliffs to your left. Return as you came.*

Continue over Slumgullion Pass on Highway 149 to Lake City. On the way, stop at the interpretive overlook for the Rio Grande River headwaters on your left and the Windy Point scenic overlook on your right—one of dozens of places with that name in Colorado. After reaching Lake City, the Hinsdale County Museum is a half-block to your left on Silver Street, which diverges at an angle from Highway 149.

Tom Boggs, Kit Carson's brother-in-law, settled in the area near Wagon Wheel Gap in 1840. A hotel opened here in 1876, and five years later, the Denver & Rio Grande opened its depot. Trains brought tourists to soak in the nearby hot springs. That depot still stands, though it is a private home.

In 1889, Nicholas Creede discovered silver ore on Willow Creek. Located at the mouth of the canyon though which Willow Creek flowed, Jim Town escaped the serious flooding that plagued camps farther up the canyon. Eventually, Jim Town inherited the name Creede. Transportation was close at hand, and the Denver & Rio Grande extended its line from Wagon Wheel Gap to Creede in 1891. Half the population of early Creede was riffraff, a who's who of troublemakers of the American West. Bob Ford. Soapy Smith. Bat Masterson. Wyatt Earp. Creede was the most lawless of the mining camps. It was here that Cy Warman, editor of the local newspaper, penned, "It's day all day in the daytime, and there is no night in Creede." A million dollars of silver left town on the railroad in 1892.

The railroad depot at Wagon Wheel Gap was still owned by the Denver & Rio Grande Railroad when this photo was taken. The concrete pier and brick rubble in the foreground are all that remain of the railroad's water tank. The depot building is now a private home.

Many of the mines at Creede are high on the slopes of Willow Creek Canyon. If you travel the Bachelor Loop, you will see why the town of Bachelor provided easy access to these aerial mines.

After rebuilding from a disastrous 1892 fire, Creede became the seat of Mineral County and structures became more substantial. Fire struck the small town again and again: in 1895, 1902, 1936, and 1946. Despite these conflagrations, there are many old structures in Creede. The Creede Historical Museum & Research Library (17 South Main Street) is located in the old railroad depot, while the Creede Underground Mining Museum (9 Forest Road 503) is appropriately built into a cliff face.

Creede survived the 1893 Silver Panic. The railroad was converted from narrow to standard width in 1902, carried passengers until 1932, and saw the last Denver & Rio Grande standard-gauge steam locomotive operation in 1952. Today, the track still exists, waiting for possible passenger service from South Fork.

Miners would have had a tough climb up the steep canyon walls atop which many of Creede's mines perched. Instead, those miners lived in the town of Bachelor, built high above Creede. Today, the unpaved Bachelor Loop tour includes the ghost town of Bachelor and the mining district. The last mine closed in 1985.

Though Creede and Lake City were served by railroads, no track ever followed the route of this journey, directly connecting the two towns via Slumgullion Pass. On your way to Lake City, you'll pass an interpretive site on the west side of the highway that overlooks the headwaters of the Rio Grande River where it begins its journey to the Gulf of Mexico. Lake City was also a mining town but was more closely associated with mining around Silverton (Journey 15) than with the mines of Creede.

Precious metals were discovered near Lake City in 1871, but mining could not begin until 1874, after the Utes ceded the land to the United States. In 1889, a narrow-gauge railroad arrived from Sapinero (Journey 12). While Creede was the most lawless of the mining camps, Lake City was the most lawful. Businessmen, ranchers, lumbermen, and other professionals moved to Lake City, intending to make it a permanent home instead of a temporary stop. Such was not to be as the mines played out, the railroad closed, and most of the town's five thousand

Trains brought building materials, mining machinery, the necessities of everyday living, and liquid comfort with which to stock saloon shelves in Creede. Those same trains also brought people: gun fighters, preachers, gamblers, prospectors, and poets. *Denver Public Library, Western History Collection, Kendrick Promotion Co., X-7476*

residents moved on. While it does not have the grandeur of more ostentatious mining camps, Lake City is a historic and scenic small town surrounded by the remnants of mining. It is home to the Hinsdale County Museum (130 North Silver Street), which sponsors walking tours of the historic district, cemetery, and historic homes. The nearby Hard Tack Mine also offers tours.

In January of 1874, Alfred Packer led five prospectors over Slumguillion Pass, starting from Montrose. That winter was severe, and Packer was not an experienced guide. Six weeks later, he appeared alone out of the wilderness, relating the story of a winter ordeal in which his companions had died. Packer did not appear underfed, and he craved whiskey, not food. A search party soon discovered that Packer's missing companions had been murdered and partially eaten! Packer disappeared but was apprehended and convicted of murder in Lake City in 1883. Packer claimed that one of the other men committed the unspeakable crimes, and Packer had killed the criminal in self-defense. After an appeal in 1886, his death sentence was reduced to forty years of hard labor. Eight years later, the *Denver Post* newspaper lobbied successfully for his pardon. Recent investigations of the crimes are still inconclusive. Packer is immortalized in song, film, and the Alfred G. Packer Memorial Grill at the University of Colorado at Boulder.

Lake San Cristobal was formed more than seven hundred years ago, when the Slumgullion earthflow dammed the Lake Fork of the Gunnison River and created Colorado's largest natural lake. The Alfred Packer Memorial stands near the turn for the lake.

The view from the Windy Point overlook near Lake City provides a spectacular panoramic view of the San Juan Mountains.

COAL COUNTRY
Around the Spanish Peaks

Conquistadors marched through the Walsenburg area searching for gold in the seventeenth century. The area was settled by Spanish farmers in 1852 and named Plaza de los Leones. Businessman Fred Walsen arrived here in 1870 and established a coal mine six years later. The town would be renamed after Walsen that year, when Colorado became a state and Walsenburg became the seat of newly formed Huerfano County. Coal production peaked in the 1930s and ended in the 1950s. Half a billion tons were removed from mines near Walsenburg. The Walsenburg Mining Museum (112 West Fifth Street) is one of the few in the state to honor coal mining, one of Colorado's major industries, and is located behind the attractive courthouse building. The old downtown is still intact and commercially viable, while the railroad depot now houses the Chamber of Commerce (400 Main Street).

Colonel John M. Francisco and Judge Henry Daigre built the Francisco Fort in the 1860s for protection from Indians and as a distribution center for agricultural products that were needed to supply the mining camps springing up west of Denver. The structure is now the Francisco Fort Museum (123 West Francisco Street) in La Veta. The Denver & Rio Grande Railroad arrived and La Veta was incorporated in 1876. The 1877 La Veta depot (132 W Ryus Avenue) still stands near the tracks. La Veta Pass passenger trains arrive and depart here.

The upper Cuchara Valley was originally settled to grow potatoes. By 1910, the first tourist cabins were built here, and Cuchara has been a tourist destination ever since. A ski area operated here intermittently from 1981 to 2000.

Your journey continues around the western side of the Spanish Peaks. The Comanche called the two almost symmetrical peaks *Wahatoya*, simply meaning "double mountain." Later, they were described as the "breasts of the world" by lonely European explorers. After cresting Cuchara Pass, you drop down into the valley of the Purgatoire River.

Stonewall was established in 1867 by Juan Guitterez and originally called El Valle del Guitterez. A 250-foot-high rock outcropping stood on land owned by James Stoner and came to be known as Stoner's Wall, from which the name of the current town was derived. A center for ranching, Stonewall also thrives on tourism for those desiring an isolated, rustic, and peaceful rest in Colorado's mountains.

DIRECTIONS

Start your journey in Walsenburg, 50 miles north of the New Mexico border on Interstate 25. Head west on U.S. Highway 160 and turn left on Colorado Highway 12 to reach La Veta. Continue through Cuchara and Stonewall.

OPTIONAL: *Turn south on unpaved County Road 13 just east of Stonewall. When you reach a "T" intersection, continue on County 13 by taking the left branch. Arrive at the gate that blocks the road just before Tercio, where you may get a glimpse of the town's large stone company store. Return the way you came and turn right on Highway 12.*

Continue following Highway 12 east to reach Weston, Segundo, and Cokedale. The latter town's coke ovens are easily visible on the south side of the highway. The town itself is north of the highway. Continue east to explore Trinidad and then drive south on Interstate 25 to the ghost town of Morley. Though you can briefly see Morley west of the interstate, take exit 2 (Wooten Road) and double back north to Morley along an unpaved frontage road. Exit 2 will also allow you to turn around to Trinidad. Ludlow is north of Trinidad along I-25. Take exit 27 and travel west to examine the Ludlow Memorial about a half mile down County Road 44.

Many of the valley's coal-producing towns were named for the Spanish words for ordinal numbers: *primero, segundo, tercio,* etc., meaning "first, second, third. . . ." There were six such locations, though some amounted to hardly more than a coal mine. A few towns had more descriptive names like Cokedale.

Tercio was the last to be built of the larger towns that had coke ovens, which were used to convert coal into coke before being transported. Looking over the fence that blocks access to Tercio—it is on private land—little is visible save the huge company store and the ruins of the coke ovens. Rows of trees mark the location of a main street, and you can imagine seeing mothers herd their children in the direction of the stone-walled store and hearing bits of conversation in English, Spanish, Italian, and several other languages you do not recognize. The Colorado & Wyoming Railroad reached Tercio in 1902; some wags nicknamed

Just east of Stonewall, this is the view from the turn on the dirt road to Terico.

its passenger train the "Spaghetti Flyer" after the Italian spoken on board. The town appeared prosperous, with 151 homes and many commercial buildings. Nevertheless, labor strife, the decline of railroads (the coal was used to produce steel to manufacture railroad rail at Pueblo), and the Great Depression spelled an end to the coal mines. Tercio and its railroad survived a while longer, but the tracks were removed in 1951, and the rails were used to build a new track along the north fork of the river to another coal mine, the Allen Mine. Even those rails were removed in the last part of the twentieth century.

Weston is a small town near the junction of the north and south forks of the Purgatoire River. The track to Tercio once headed south from Weston, and the track to the Allen Mine traveled westward from here. A row of small, identical homes identify Weston as a company town, built by the mining firm.

The coal washer is on the left, and the tipple for loading railroad cars on the right in this photo of just a small portion of the industrial plant once located at Segundo. *Colorado Historical Society, Dold & Peacock, CHS.X4908*

Huge coke ovens were constructed at Segundo. Much of the coal from mines at Weston and Primero was converted to coke at Segundo before being transported to the steel mill at Pueblo. The shops of the Colorado & Wyoming Railroad were located here, and a railroad bridge, the depot (now a private home), and the turntable survived the railroad's removal. It is a quiet town, much smaller than it once was. During the Industrial Revolution it must have been a hellish place where smoke muted the sun during the day, a red glow reflected off the clouds at night, and noise assaulted the ears at all hours as trains squealed around tight curves and machinery whirred.

Cokedale was the final thriving coal-mining town in the valley. The last of three mines, the Bon Carbo, and the coke ovens closed in 1947 leaving *12 square miles* of mined-out rooms beneath the surface. Residents of the company-owned town were given one month's notice to leave. Many decided to purchase their homes and stay. Today, a portion of Cokedale—the best preserved of all Colorado's coal-mining towns—is known as the Cokedale Historic District. It is located on the north side of Colorado Highway 12, while extensive coke ovens can be seen on the south side. Cokedale was once so prosperous that its residents could ride the Trinidad Electric Railway, a trolley, into downtown Trinidad.

The New Elk Mine, formerly the Allen Mine, was closed in 1996. Shortly afterwards, the Colorado & Wyoming's tracks were removed from most of the Purgatoire River valley.

Felipe and Dolores Baca settled at Trinidad in 1861 along with others migrating from New Mexico. Trinidad was incorporated in 1876, just months before Colorado became a state. Frank and Sarah Bloom built their mansion here in 1882. Their home is now the Bloom Mansion museum, part of the Trinidad History Museum complex (312 East Main Street), which also includes the Baca House and Santa Fe Trail Museum.

BEFORE THE UNITED STATES EXPANDED its borders to the Pacific Ocean, ownership of the West was claimed by Spain, France, and Britain. The region that became Colorado was divided between the French in its east and the Spanish in its west. It was the Spanish who mounted the most aggressive exploration and colonization efforts, so it is the Spanish who are most remembered for their discoveries in Colorado.

Conquistador Francisco Coronado mounted an enormous expedition to discover the rumored Seven Cities of Cebolla and the gold they contained. He failed to find gold but nicked the southeastern corner of Colorado in 1541 on his return southward. The expedition was a failure, and Coronado never regained the status he once enjoyed.

Don Juan de Oñate Salazar was born in Zacatecas, New Spain—now Mexico—and eventually became its governor. In 1595, under orders from King Phillip II of Spain, he began to colonize the upper Rio Grande valley. Some of his expedition's members penetrated Colorado's San Luis Valley (Journey 16). He planned the city of Santa Fe but was relieved of his command after being accused of murdering, maiming, and enslaving Native Americans.

In 1765, explorer Juan Maria Antonio Rivera led an expedition into Colorado's southern mountains, looking for gold in an effort to thwart the ambitions of other European powers in the area. He traveled as far west as Utah.

Fathers Francisco Atanasio Dominguez and Silvestre Velez de Escalante mounted an expedition in 1776 to find a route from Santa Fe to the Spanish missions of California. They may have been the first Europeans to spot Mesa Verde. The two pueblo ruins along the trail at the Anasazi Heritage Center (Journey 13) are named for these explorers.

Though his explorations were mainly in Arizona and California, Juan Bautista de Anza became governor of Nuevo Mexico—New Mexico—in 1777. He pursued hostile Comanche Indians into the San Luis Valley in 1779. Doggedly continuing through the Manitou Springs area (Journey 21), he found a small Comanche party in what is now Colorado Springs (Journey 20), followed them down to the area of Pueblo (Journey 22), and inflicted a decisive defeat on the main force of Comanches he found there.

Francisco Vasquez de Coronado led the earliest European expedition into the American West and touched what is now Colorado in 1541. *Library of Congress, Remington Drawing, LC-USZ62-37993*

Combining sandstone and brick, this commercial block is one of many substantial structures in Trinidad's historic downtown. There are also churches, theaters, and industrial buildings.

Trindad's historic downtown is a gem. Whether you just walk around the historic district or take a summer guided tour on the Trinidad Trolley (available at the Colorado Welcome Center and all the museums), it will be time well spent. The town was prosperous culturally as well as commercially; beautiful, substantial buildings line the streets. Associated with Spanish settlement, Trinidad also hosted mountain man Kit Carson and gunfighters Bat Masterson and Wyatt Earp, as well German, Irish, Jewish, Polish, Italian, and Chinese coal miners. Trinidad State Junior College is the oldest public two-year college in Colorado.

In 1821, William Becknell made the first recorded trading trip over what became known as the mountain branch of the Santa Fe Trail, which passed through the location that became Trinidad and over Raton Pass. To ease the difficult journey over Raton Pass, Richard Lacy "Uncle Dick" Wooten built a toll road over the pass in 1865, and in 1876, 15,000 tons of freight traveled over the road. Raton Pass means "Pass of the Rat"—a prophetic name, as the Santa Fe Railway was to secure the route and exclude the Denver & Rio Grande by treachery in the late 1870s. Blocked from its proposed route to Mexico City, the Denver & Rio Grande Railroad made the fateful decision to build into Colorado's mountains, first completing the line to Alamosa. Colorado's mountain history would not be as interesting without that single act of deception.

South of Trinidad on Raton Pass, you can spot the ruins of St. Aloysius Church on a hillside west of Interstate Highway 25. This was the site of Morely. Mounds of black diamonds are a sure clue that Morley was a coal-mining town. Coal was discovered here in 1906, and the original town moved about a mile south to nestle up to the coal mines. Morley's mines closed after World War II, as

The Southern Colorado Coal Miners Memorial stands in downtown Trinidad with the spire of the Holy Trinity Catholic Church in the distance.

Fisher's Peak overlooks downtown Trinidad in 1907. Trinidad was a significant town early in Colorado's history, unusual for a city that relied on neither gold nor silver for its economy. *Library of Congress, A. R. Arlen, LC-USZ62-112780*

did many in the area. You'll have only a quick look from the highway, but imagine one hundred homes, a company store, a grade school, the obligatory saloon, a hotel, and, of course, worshippers filing into St. Aloysius on Sunday.

Take a short side trip north of Trinidad to see Ludlow. As the nineteenth century became the twentieth, immigrants from Europe and Asia arrived to work Colorado's many coal camps. One of those camps was Ludlow. By 1913, it had a population of one thousand and a significant commercial district. Like most coal-mining towns, Ludlow was a company town. Miners were paid in company scrip instead of money, and the scrip could be used only at company-owned stores, making it difficult or impossible for miners to quit and leave. This practice, plus the incredibly dangerous and difficult work of underground coal mining, brought the United Mine Workers to the area. On September 23, 1913, the miners went on strike. Since the towns were owned by the mining companies, families relocated to tent colonies nearby. One such colony was north of Ludlow. A real shooting war followed.

In the upper left of this photo is the ruined St. Aloysius church at the ghost town of Morley. The blackness of coal in the lower right clearly identifies the mineral removed from the earth here.

On April 20, 1914, bullets split the air. There is still disagreement about who fired first. Two women and eleven children ran to hide in a storage pit dug beneath a tent. The tent town caught fire. One can only imagine the horror as the women hugged the terrified, crying children. All were found dead the next morning, clutching each other and asphyxiated by smoke from the fires. Five striking miners, two more young children, and four militiamen were also dead.

Battles at more coal camps followed, taking many more lives. Federal troops finally arrived and restored peace. The strike ended, unresolved. It was the beginning of a long, slow process of improving miners' working conditions. In 1918, a stone memorial was erected here by the United Mine Workers of America. A few buildings remained after the mines closed in the 1950s, and the entire 40-acre site is now on the National Historic Register.

DIRECTIONS

This journey starts in Rocky Ford on U.S. Highway 50 east of Pueblo. Drive eastward on U.S. 50 and turn left on Colorado Highway 109. Turn right on Colorado Highway 194 to reach Bent's Old Fort. Continue eastward and turn right, via a ramp, onto westbound U.S. 50 (Bent Avenue) to reach Las Animas. In Las Animas, follow U.S. 50 as it turns to the west and becomes 7th Street. Immediately after this bend, turn left on Colorado Highway 101 (Carson Avenue). You will reach Boggsville on your left in about a mile. Retrace your steps and turn right on U.S. 50 (7th Street). Fort Lyon is on a short stub road. Follow U.S. 50 through Lamar to reach Granada. Go north on U.S. Highway 385 and turn left on Colorado Highway 96.

Turn right on County Road 54 and then right on County Road W. Continue to the Sand Creek Massacre National Historic Site. Retrace your steps and continue west on Highway 96 to reach Eads. Turn right at U.S. Highway 287 (Wansted Street). U.S. 287 curves to the west and takes you into Kit Carson. Return eastward on U.S. 287, but immediately take the turn onto eastbound U.S. Highway 40 to reach Cheyenne Wells. The Cheyenne Wells streets are a little confusing. From U.S. 40, turn left on West 6th Street, and then turn right after the railroad tracks onto South 2nd Street. Turn left onto U.S. Highway 385.

Follow U.S. 385 north to Burlington, where this highway becomes Lincoln Street. Stay on U.S. 385 by turning right onto Rose Street. Turn right on 14th Street to reach the Old Town Museum. The Kit Carson County Carousel is located at the County Fairgrounds, north on 15th Street. Return southbound on U.S. 385 to enter Interstate 70 westbound. From I-70's exit 361, follow Main Street west into Limon. Turn left on E Avenue to reach the Limon Heritage Museum & Railroad Park and the end of your journey.

The existing Rocky Ford depot was constructed by the Santa Fe Railway in 1907. Where other railroads' small depots often used standardized designs of nondescript architecture, the Santa Fe frequently designed unique structures with southwestern motifs. Rocky Ford's brick depot included a Venetian tile roof to enhance the Spanish architectural theme.

SOUTHWESTERN SUPERHIGHWAY

THE SANTA FE TRAIL was a main route of commerce in the web of trails draped over the western American continent. It began in Missouri and wound its way west to Santa Fe, then part of Mexico and now the second oldest city in the United States. Mexico won independence from Spain in 1821, and the U.S. government arranged to survey the trail in 1825. After the United States and Mexico waged war from 1846 to 1848, Mexico surrendered much of what is now the southwestern United States, including the western portion of the trail.

The 1849 California gold rush soon increased traffic on the Santa Fe Trail as fledgling prospectors headed west to make their fortunes. During the trail's peak popularity, there were several alternate routes along its length, but the traveler's main decision was whether to take the shorter Cimarron Route though Oklahoma's panhandle or the safer Mountain Route though Colorado.

Two decades later, the nation's first transcontinental railroad was completed. Although it was built far north of the Santa Fe Trail, many long-distance travelers abandoned their rickety wagons for the comfort and speed of trains. Other railroads quickly followed in a mad dash westward. One, the Atchison, Topeka & Santa Fe, followed a route almost parallel to the Santa Fe Trail, hastening the trail's decline into obscurity. The entire route is now the Santa Fe National Historic Trail of the National Park Service. The Santa Fe Trail Association works to preserve its history. Present-day explorers travel along bits of the trail.

Trinidad was on the mountain branch of the Old Santa Fe Trail, and trail pioneer Kit Carson was honored there at the dedication of Kit Carson Park and the Kit Carson Statue on June 1, 1913. Carson's daughter and two of his granddaughters attended the celebration. *Library of Congress, Almeron Newman, PAN SUBJECT-Events No. 127*

La Junta means "The Junction." True to the name, the Santa Fe Railway paused here in late 1875. From junctions nearby, Santa Fe trains could eventually travel east to Chicago or Dodge City, south to Amarillo and Albuquerque, or west to Pueblo and then north to Denver. The connecting Arkansas Valley Railroad provided access to the Kansas Pacific's tracks at the town of Kit Carson. La Junta nearly vanished until the Santa Fe decided to construct major shops here in 1879. The town was incorporated in 1881, a child of the Santa Fe Railway and not the Santa Fe Trail. Many of its substantial historic structures still exist.

The Santa Fe Railway contracted its restaurant operations to Fred Harvey, who created an epicurean empire known for great food, fast service, and attractive, young waitresses. It was an unbeatable combination in the rugged American West. The La Junta Hotel and Raiload Eating House was a substantial addition to La Junta's 1882 skyline.
Denver Public Library, Western History Collection, X-10478

The first meeting of a Boy Scout Indian Club, the Koshares, was called to order in La Junta in February of 1933. The Koshare Indian Museum (115 West 18th Street) preserves Native American artifacts and culture, and the Koshare Indian Dancers perform there. The Otero Museum (706 West 3rd Street) chronicles the history of the area.

Bent's Old Fort National Historic Site is an accurate reconstruction of the famous trading post operated by Charles and William Bent along the route of the Santa Fe Trail. The original was constructed in 1833 and prospered for sixteen years as a center for the fur trade, spearheading U.S. expansion into the western continent. The large facility hosts seasonal living-history demonstrations and other events.

Downtown Las Animas offers several significant historic buildings, including the active Bent County Courthouse (725 Bent Avenue) and the inactive Santa Fe train depot (8th Street and Bent Avenue). The Kit Carson Museum

Living-history programs are hosted at Bent's Old Fort National Historic Site in busier seasons. The current structure was constructed on the ruins of the original post.

(9th Street and Bent Avenue) chronicles local history from the days of the famous frontiersman. Boggsville, a restored site just south of Las Animas, was the last home of Carson as well as one of the first nonmilitary settlements in southeastern Colorado. Named after a ranch established by Thomas Boggs in 1862, the site was first visited by Zebulon Pike in 1806 and has a long history of European activity.

Stroll with Kit Carson down the streets of Boggsville. Perhaps he stops to visit at the Boggs home, constructed in 1866, or the Prowers home, built in 1867, both of which still grace the grove of trees that once sheltered Carson as he walked. You can easily see the Santa Fe Trail where its marked route passes through Boggsville, but you'll have to imagine pioneer covered wagons as they rolled westward. For a brief period after 1870, Boggsville became Bent County's seat, serving 576 individuals scattered over 5,500 square miles. A nearby bridge over the Arkansas River and the arrival of the Santa Fe Railway at the present site of Las Animas spelled doom for Boggsville by about 1880.

William Bent abandoned his old fort in 1852 and moved 30 miles east, where he built a smaller outpost overlooking the Arkansas River in 1853. Some say he blew up or burned down the old fort in anger over not being able to sell it to the

Thomas Boggs began construction of an adobe home in 1866, south of present-day Las Animas. Eventually, the small town named Boggsville developed at this location, through which the Santa Fe Trail passes. Preserved here are the original Boggs and two-story Prowers houses.

U.S. government. William Bent leased his new stone fort to the government in 1857 for storage of supplies by its Indian agent. In 1860, the U.S. Army built Fort Wise—renamed Fort Lyon a year after construction—near Bent's New Fort for the protection of settlers.

New Fort Lyon soon replaced the older fort, which was subject to flooding. Kit Carson died at new Fort Lyon of an aortic aneurysm on May 23, 1868. Abandoned by the U.S. Army in 1897, the fort became a U.S. Navy tuberculosis hospital and then a Veteran's Bureau hospital in 1922. Currently, it is a minimum-security Colorado prison. Military burials started here with U.S. Navy stewardship, and the cemetery became Fort Lyon National Cemetery in 1973.

Lamar was a town instantly created when the Santa Fe Railway moved its depot from Blackwell to Lamar, three miles farther west, on May 24, 1886, in response to a dispute with cattleman A. R. Black, who had refused to donate land for a town site. The Lamar Chamber of Commerce (109A East Beech Street) occupies a historic Santa Fe depot, though it is not the same building that was moved from Blackwell. Lamar's Big Timbers Museum (7515 U.S. Highway 50) includes, among other interesting exhibits, one that documents a darker side of

Lamar's residents conducted business in this ornamented brick commercial block in the 1890s. The brick structure's signage indicates that it shelters a bank, a hardware store, and a druggist, while the frame structure to the right houses a real estate office. *Denver Public Library, Western History Collection, X-11968*

American history, Camp Amache—one of several camps that housed Americans of Japanese descent during World War II. Anyone of Japanese ancestry—U.S. citizen and non-citizen alike—was seen as a security risk on the West Coast, where the Japanese immigrant population lived, so the government forced their removal. Camp Amache, at one time the tenth-largest city in Colorado, was near the present town of Granada.

Old Fort Lyon also has a dark history. It was from here that Colonel John Chivington set out to attack Cheyenne and Arapaho Indians camped along Sand Creek. On the morning of November 29, 1864, seven hundred soldiers descended on the camp. Small bands of soldiers continued to hunt and kill Indians the entire day, and by the end, 160 Indians—many women, children, and elderly—lay dead. Three hundred escaped. Chivington's actions were condemned by two Congressional committees soon afterward. The Sand Creek Massacre National Historic Site, north of Lamar, now commemorates this sad event in American history.

Eads is one of several towns that appeared as the Missouri Pacific Railroad started its march westward from the Kansas border to Pueblo in 1887. Eads

There could be no more classic image of eastern Colorado than a grain elevator standing by a railroad track—an example of which is shown at Eads.

became the seat of Kiowa County in 1902. By 1904, the population of the Eads area was sixty-seven people, ten of whom worked for the railroad. The Kiowa County Historical Museum (1313 Maine Street) is in Eads. Small and off a major highway, Eads is a great example of the remarkable pride that many, perhaps most, agricultural towns take in themselves.

The town of Kit Carson was once a trading post established by the legendary trapper, explorer, and Indian fighter. It is an agricultural town with a sprinkling of oil wells, and its wonderful museum (Park Street and U.S. 287)—one of two in Colorado named the Kit Carson Museum—reflects this dual heritage. Indoor exhibits are housed in a beautifully restored 1904 railroad depot. Outdoor exhibit areas include a number of outhouses, a unique collection if ever there was one. Some artifacts are familiar, but others, such as the scrap-metal sculpture created by welder Red Moreland, are not.

By this point in your journeys, you've surely identified the importance of railroads to Colorado's settlements, and the town of Kit Carson is no exception. The Kansas Pacific Railway was completed from Kansas City to Denver in 1870 and became part of the Union Pacific, whose trains still rumble through town today.

The Cheyenne County Museum (85 West 2nd Street) is housed in an old county jail in Cheyenne Wells. The jail's unusual structure was designed in 1892 by architect Robert S. Roeschlaub, who also designed the Central City Opera House and Denver's Trinity United Methodist Church (Journey 7).

You'll reach the tracks of yet another east-west railroad at Burlington. The railroad, its depot, and the town all appeared in 1888. The Chicago, Rock Island & Pacific was the quintessential agricultural railroad, wandering over the nation's heartland from grain elevator to grain elevator. In 1980, more than 7,000 miles of the "The Rock" fell silent as the railroad's bankruptcy took hold, the largest railroad demise in U.S. history. Burlington's railroad is now operated by shortline operator Kyle Railways.

The historic centerpiece of Burlington is the Old Town Museum (420 South 14th Street). Its six and a half acres include a large building that houses indoor exhibits as well as a huge outdoor exhibit area featuring twenty-one stunningly restored or reconstructed buildings. Seasonal activities include a can-can show and a wagon ride to the Kit Carson County Carousel (815 North 15 Street). Burlington is the county seat, and the magnificent restored carousel, hand carved by the Philadelphia Toboggan Company in 1905, enlivens the county fair grounds. Open summer afternoons, the Kit Carson County Carousel recalls the

An ironically labeled horse-drawn wagon delivered fuel for newfangled motor cars. The barber shop in the background is one of twenty restored or reconstructed historic buildings located on the six and a half acres of Burlington's Old Town Museum.

simpler, more relaxed entertainment of a bygone era. A museum interprets the history and the restoration of the carousel.

At first, Limon was only a camp for workers building the Rock Island Railroad in 1888. John Limon was a construction supervisor for that railroad. After the Rock Island reached Colorado Springs, the railroad decided that Denver was a better destination for its western terminus. Limon became an important junction when the railroad built a second track that diverged here to continue northwest to Denver. The Limon Heritage Museum and Railroad Park (899 1st Street) includes exhibits on local history as well as railroad history. There are full-sized railroad cars, a large depot, model railroads, great historic photographs, and much more.

LITTLE LONDON
Under America's Mountain

The Colorado Springs metropolitan area is the second largest in Colorado. Nestled against the eastern slopes of Pikes Peak, it has been Colorado's premier tourist destination for over a century. Unlike much of pioneer Colorado, it developed as an elegant and refined place and, for the most part, lacked the gunfights, saloons, and brothels of the mountain mining towns. (It supplied those towns but did not partake of their recreational activities!) On the dividing line between mountain and plain, it also identified with agriculture to the east. It was a residential town for the wealthy, a tourist destination for the adventurous, and a supply center for southern Colorado.

Colorado Springs was founded by General William Jackson Palmer in 1871 as a gentile town with an educated and enlightened citizenry. Not until the 1933 repeal of prohibition was alcohol permitted. Palmer also built the original Antlers Hotel. The Antlers Hilton Hotel (4 South Cascade Avenue) still welcomes guests, though they relax in the third building on this spot. Nearby is the original Denver & Rio Grande depot, which at one time also saw trains of the Rock Island Railroad but now hosts diners in Giuseppe's Old Depot Restaurant (10 South Sierra Madre Street). The Santa Fe's passenger depot (555 East Pikes Peak Avenue) also saw trains of the legendary Colorado Midland and is now part of an office complex.

DIRECTIONS

A Colorado Springs street map will be essential. There is no particular order in which you should visit the places mentioned in the journey, especially those near downtown, Garden of the Gods, and the Broadmoor.

From Colorado Springs, travel north on Interstate 25 and west on North Gate Boulevard, exit 156B, to reach the Air Force Academy gate used by visitors. Return toward the interstate but continue east on North Gate Boulevard to the Western Museum of Mining and Industry on your right. Return south on I-25. The ProRodeo Hall of Fame and Museum of the American Cowboy will be at exit 147, Rockrimmon Boulevard.

Continue south on I-25 to exit 145, Fillmore Street. Travel east a short distance to Steele Drive and turn right to reach the Pikes Peak Historical Street Railway Foundation Museum. Retrace your path to I-25 and continue south. Take exit 141, U.S. Highway 24 (Cimarron Street) westbound. Turn south on 21st Street and then right immediately past the Colorado Midland roundhouse. This is the driveway that serves the roundhouse and the Ghost Town Museum. Return north on 21st Street. Cross U.S. 24 and turn left on Colorado Avenue. Turn right on 24th Street. The Old Colorado History Center will be one block down on your right. Continue west on Colorado Avenue. If you have yet to see the Garden of the Gods, you can turn right on 30th Street to reach it.

Drive west on Colorado Avenue to reach downtown Manitou Springs, where Colorado Avenue is rechristened Manitou Avenue. Turn left on Ruxton Avenue to reach the Manitou & Pikes Peak Railway depot. Return to Manitou Avenue, make a right turn back to U.S. 24, and move into the left lane to enter that highway westbound. You will encounter the Cliff Dwellings entrance on the right. Slightly farther west will be the Cave of the Winds, also on your right. A Manitou Springs street map would be an excellent idea; many Colorado Springs street maps also include Manitou Springs.

The second Antlers Hotel building is shown here in 1908. A maze of overhead wires powers the electric trolley cars that provided excellent public transportation in Colorado Springs until 1932. *Library of Congress, Detroit Publishing Company, LC-USZ62-78480*

COLORADO INDUSTRIALIST

WILLIAM JACKSON PALMER'S 1870 arrival in Colorado would be pivotal to its development. Palmer became the pioneer industrialist who drove railroad tracks into the mountains, founded cities, and built industries. His activities influenced history throughout the state.

Palmer was born in Delaware to a Quaker family but moved to Pennsylvania as a child, where he entered railroad service at age seventeen. He traveled to Europe to study railroads and returned to rise in the ranks of the Pennsylvania Railroad. He served in the Civil War and, like many veterans, traveled west to seek his fortune after the war. Railroads had a large, dispersed workforce; the military provided the only similar management model, so military officers often obtained positions with railroads. Palmer was put in charge of locating the Kansas Pacific Railway to Denver.

Palmer married Mary Lincoln "Queen" Mellen on November 8, 1870. Having seen narrow-gauge railroads on his honeymoon in Britain, he started construction of his own Denver & Rio Grande Railroad as a narrow-gauge artery intended to link Denver with Mexico City. He founded the city of Colorado Springs (Journey 20) in 1871 and built a steel mill at Pueblo (Journey 22) in 1879.

Palmer built his home at Colorado Springs and named it Glen Eyrie, meaning "Eagle's Nest." He and Queen had three daughters. Queen suffered a mild heart attack in 1880 and was advised to move to a lower elevation, first to the eastern United States and then to England. General Palmer continued to live in Colorado Springs to direct his industrial empire and visited his remote family as often as possible. Queen died just a few days after Christmas in 1894. She was only forty-four years old. After 1901, William Palmer spent his retirement years as a benefactor to Colorado Springs. An avid horseman, he was paralyzed in a fall in 1906 and passed away in Glen Eyrie in 1909 at the age of seventy-two.

In 1809, General Palmer relaxes in his Glen Eyrie home, located in Queens Canyon, north of the Garden of the Gods. Glen Eyrie still exists and is home to a Christian organization. *Denver Public Library, Western History Collection, X-14703*

So many English visitors arrived to enjoy both the healthy, dry climate and the spectacular Pikes Peak view that the town earned the nickname "Little London." This old, elegant part of Colorado Springs is most visible north of downtown in the residential neighborhoods on Wood and Cascade avenues. Here, you'll also find the McAllister House (423 North Cascade Avenue), a restored home open for tours.

The McAllister House is a small home north of downtown Colorado Springs built by Henry McAllister in 1873, only two years after the founding of Colorado Springs. It features many original furnishings and three marble fireplaces.

Colorado's last gold rush, which took place on the western slope of Pikes Peak, brought even more wealth to Colorado Springs. Rough and ready miners often ended their lives in the more civilized Colorado Springs, and some became great benefactors. Winfield Scott Stratton was responsible for a superb trolley system that served the city's public transportation needs. He donated money and land for various civic projects, including the spectacular El Paso County Courthouse, which now houses the Colorado Springs Pioneers Museum (215 South Tejon Street). Ride—or even drive—a streetcar at the Pikes Peak Historical Street Railway Foundation museum at the old Rock Island roundhouse (2333 Steel Drive).

Spencer Penrose, with his partner, Charles Tutt, extracted a great fortune from the mines of the Cripple Creek & Victor Mining District (Journey 21). Penrose purchased the Broadmoor Hotel (1 Lake Avenue) in Colorado Springs and developed it into the five-star destination resort you see today. Walk though the main building and around the lake, enjoy a meal in one of the restaurants, or even stay a few nights in an elegant room. Visit the Cheyenne Mountain Zoo

(4250 Cheyenne Mountain Zoo Road), which was originally built by Penrose as a private collection for himself and his Broadmoor guests. An elegant residential neighboorhood developed around the hotel and was eventually annexed into Colorado Springs. After Penrose died, his good works continued in the form of the El Pomar Foundation under the Tutt family's leadership of that organization.

Colorado Springs retains its appeal as a vacation destination. The ProRodeo Hall of Fame and Museum of the American Cowboy (101 ProRodeo Drive) chronicles the sport of rodeo. The U.S. Air Force Academy, Colorado's top-ranked tourist destination, has a large and informative visitors' center (2346 Academy Drive). Learn about nineteenth-century mining technology at the Western Museum of Mining and Industry (1025 Northgate Road, across from the Air Force Academy's north entrance).

The United States Air Force Academy is adjacent to Colorado Springs's northern border. The dorms, classroom, and cadet-related buildings are clustered near the northwestern corner of the facility, which opened in 1958. Here you will also find a large, informative visitors' center. The tall triangular building is the Cadet Chapel.

Old Colorado City (the neighborhood in Colorado Springs, not the Colorado City on Interstate 25 south of Pueblo) became the hub of industrial activity in the area. Workmen lived here with their families. Wagons loaded with supplies traveled up Ute Pass. Later, the Colorado Midland Railway built its tracks from Colorado City up Ute Pass (Journey 21); across windswept South Park and over Trout Creek Pass; to Buena Vista and Leadville and over Hagerman Pass (Journey 10); to Basalt, Aspen, and Glenwood Springs (Journey 2); and finally down the Colorado River to Grand Junction (Journey 1). Construction began in 1886, and it was the first standard-gauge railroad to cross Colorado's mountains. It was dismantled in 1921 and was the first major U.S. railroad to be abandoned in what would become an all-too-common story.

Colorado City was eventually folded into Colorado Springs and is a historic commercial and residential neighborhood worth visiting. You'll find the huge stone Colorado Midland roundhouse (600 South 21st Street) still standing at the corner of 21st Street and U.S. Highway 24. The Ghost Town Museum (400 South 21st Street), across the parking lot from the roundhouse, was the Colorado Midland Railway's machine shop. Attractive and interesting exhibits decorate the Old Colorado City History Center (1 South 24th Street) near Bancroft Park. Bancroft Park is a classic old-time venue for summer concerts adjacent to the historic Old Colorado City shopping district.

The Colorado Midland Railway band provides summertime entertainment, possibly in Bancroft Park in Old Colorado City, in 1908. In less than a decade, the Colorado Midland would be no more, and these amateur bandsmen would no longer be employed on the railroad. *Library of Congress, H. T. Irvine, LC-USZ62-120308*

In 1879, Charles Elliot Perkins, the head of the Burlington Railroad, purchased 240 acres of red-rock monoliths that had once been the site of Cheyenne, Arapaho, and Ute Indian encampments. Perkins died in 1907, and his children, following their father's wishes, donated the enlarged 480-acre site to the City of Colorado Springs to become the Garden of the Gods. Today, greatly expanded, it may be the most spectacular city park anywhere in the nation. There is a

visitors' center (1805 North 30th Street at Gateway Road) that explains both the human and natural history of the park. The Rock Ledge Ranch Historic Site (off Gateway Road just west of 30th Street), with its Orchard House, adjoins the Garden of the Gods. The Orchard House's 1938 white stucco covering inspired the nickname "White House Ranch," which is still sometimes used. Today Rock Ledge Ranch is a living-history museum.

Pikes Peak looms over Gateway Rocks in Garden of the Gods, the immensely impressive Colorado Springs city park.

The Garden of the Gods' giant, red sandstone formations are pictured in this vintage postcard.

567   THE THREE GRACES, GARDEN OF THE GODS

COLORADO SPRINGS, COLORADO   14430

Two dozen bubbling springs attracted the aching bones of Ute, Arapaho, Cheyenne, and Kiowa Indians to the foot of Ute Pass. Dr. William Bell, an associate of General William Palmer, saw potential for a great city here, a European-style spa with grand hotels, extravagant homes, and elegant public spaces. He built a mansion for himself, now the Briarhurst Manor restaurant (404 Manitou Avenue). His dream failed to materialize in quite the way he envisioned, but eventually Manitou Springs became a popular health resort and evolved into the tourist destination it is today.

Of the many elegant Manitou Springs hotels, two structures remain: the Barker House (819 Manitou Avenue) and the Cliff House (306 Cañon Avenue). The Cliff House is hidden away not far from the main shopping district, and it is worth your time to find this beautifully restored historic hotel or perhaps spend your stay here. Manitou's Cave of the Winds (U.S. Highway 24 and Cave of the Winds Road) is one of only two public "show caves" in Colorado. The other is in Glenwood Springs (Journey 4). The Cliff Dwellings Museum (U.S. Highway 24 and Cliff Dwellings Road) is a reconstruction of the type of dwelling found at Mesa Verde (Journey 13). A century ago, it was an arduous days-long adventure to reach Mesa Verde, so Manitou Springs brought the cliff dwellings to its visitors.

Zalmon Simmons, who manufactured mattresses in Wisconsin, was convinced to fund the construction of a railroad in Manitou Springs after he suffered through a painful round-trip burro ride to Pikes Peak's summit. In 1891, Simmon's cog railroad, which uses a toothed center rail to climb steep inclines, was completed from Manitou Springs to the very pinnacle of Pikes Peak. The Manitou & Pike's Peak Railway (515 Ruxton Avenue) is the highest cog railroad in the world, the highest railroad of any kind in North America, and the third-highest railroad of any kind in the world. It still carries passengers to the summit of Pikes Peak.

A vintage postcard depicts the Manitou resort area, nestled at the base of Pikes Peak.

Today's passengers usually arrive at the summit of Pikes Peak in modern Swiss-built trains. Some lucky passengers book special historic excursions on this 1950s-era diesel streamliner.

Catholic clergyman Father Jean Baptiste Francolon moved to Manitou Springs from Santa Fe, New Mexico, in the early 1890s, hoping that the mineral waters would alleviate his abdominal distress. In 1895, he donated his original residence to the Sisters of Mercy for use as the Montcalme Sanitarium and began work on the stone castle that would become his home. The spectacular castle was completed in 1896 and houses the 14,000-square-foot Miramont Castle Museum (9 Capitol Hill Avenue), which chronicles local history.

LAST RUSH
In the Shadow of America's Mountain

Ute Indians traveled west over the pass that now bears the tribe's name. Later, European explorers also trudged up Ute Pass. Commerce with the South Park mining towns was conducted by horse-drawn wagon before the trains of the Colorado Midland Railway chugged into the mountains via this same passage.

The Cascade town company was formed in 1886, shortly after plans for the railroad were announced. Construction of the elegant Ramona Hotel began in 1888, as Cascade and other Ute Pass towns became high-elevation escapes from the summer heat. That same year, the Pikes Peak toll road was completed from Cascade to the summit of "America's mountain." Permanent summer residences appeared, including Marigreen Pines, the mansion of Thomas Cusack. Now a religious community, the mansion will be above the stone wall on your right as you drive into Cascade. The Ramona Hotel is no more, but many other historic buildings, especially older residences, still enjoy the coolness of summer.

In 1890, the Ute Pass Land and Water Company began development of a summer resort community, which would become Chipita Park. Cottages surrounded the Ute Hotel, which hovered over a red sandstone railroad depot and a manmade lake. Little development occurred until Frank Marcroft gained control of the company in 1927, named the community Chipita Park (after Chipeta, the wife of Chief Ouray, whose story is told in Chapter 4), and aggressively promoted land sales.

In contrast, promotion of Green Mountain Falls began in 1887 as soon as railroad access was assured. Streets were built along with the mandatory real-estate office. The Green Mountain Falls Hotel opened in 1889. A manmade lake featured an island on which a gazebo was built. Railroad excursions brought visitors, hundreds at a time. Circus entrepreneur P. T. Barnum had a summer home here. Hybrid tents decorated the hillsides: Their canvas tops were removed every autumn and replaced on their log bottoms every spring to prepare for the onslaught of fair-weather visitors. Today, the hotel is gone, as are all the grand old Ute Pass hotels. The lake and its gazebo are the most recognizable remnants of the early history of Ute Pass, and the railroad grade is now a path on the side of the lake opposite the road. A little farther west, the Church of the Wildwood still incorporates the portion of that structure built in 1889.

PIKES PEAK PIONEER

CITIES, COUNTIES, A NATIONAL FOREST, warships, and America's most famous mountain are named for Zebulon Pike. His fame is justified by his very early missions of exploration into the American West. As a U.S. Army lieutenant, he commanded two expeditions into the mostly unexplored Louisiana Territory, recently purchased from France. On the first of these, in 1805, he traced the Mississippi River to its source. On the second, in 1806, Pike left St. Louis with twenty-six men to explore the Arkansas River. He sighted the mountain that would bear his name on November 15, 1806. Attempting to climb the peak, he was turned back by excessive snow and declared that no one would ever climb it, overestimating its height at 18,581 feet. Fourteen years later, Dr. Edwin James stood on Pikes Peak's summit; a trail was completed in 1852; the first woman, Julia Holmes, climbed it in 1858; and a railroad reached the top in 1891 (Journey 21)!

Pike's adventures did not end with the mountain. He trespassed into Spanish territory and was taken into custody in the San Luis Valley (Journey 16) by the Spanish but was quickly freed. (He was, in fact, under army orders to spy on Spanish settlements in the area.) Pike was promoted to captain in 1806 and to major in 1808, and he advanced to colonel early in the War of 1812 with Great Britain. Finally, as a brigadier general, he commanded a successful attack on Toronto, Canada, and was killed by an explosion during that attack in 1813.

The sign on their wagon likely indicates these men are participating in the first Colorado gold rush, which actually took place west of Denver, some distance from Pikes Peak. Nevertheless, all of Colorado—and frequently all of the American West—was identified with Pikes Peak, the easternmost peak of the Rockies. *Denver Public Library, Western History Collection, X-21803*

DIRECTIONS

Drive west from Manitou Springs on U.S. Highway 24. Turn right at the stoplight in Cascade (Topeka Avenue). When you are done exploring, return on Topeka and cross U.S. 24 at that stoplight. In about a quarter-mile, turn right on the Chipita Park Road, which becomes Ute Pass Avenue in Green Mountain Falls. Continue and turn left at U.S. 24. Crystola will be a small cluster of buildings on your left. In Woodland Park, turn right on Fairview to reach the Ute Pass Cultural Center and its adjacent History Park. Return to westbound U.S. 24 to reach Divide, where you will turn left on Colorado Highway 67.

Stop at the parking area for the Waters Tunnel and then continue through Gillette. Before you reach Cripple Creek, you will pass the Mollie Kathleen Gold Mine and the Pikes Peak Heritage Center. Turn left into the parking lot of the Cripple Creek District Museum. The Cripple Creek & Victor Narrow Gauge Railroad is immediately adjacent to the museum. To reach the Old Homestead House brothel, return to Highway 67 (west on Bennett Avenue) and turn left on 4th Street. Drive one block to Myers Avenue and the Old Homestead House. Return and continue westbound on Bennett Avenue. Turn left on 2nd Street, Highway 67, toward Victor.

After exploring Victor, continue on Highway 67 (north on 3rd Street and right on Diamond Avenue). Still in town, take the road to your left to the American Eagles Mine and return the way you came to turn left on Highway 67. Turn left again on County Road 81 to reach Goldfield. Goldfield will be on your right, and the Vindicator Valley trailhead parking area is near here on your left. Continue on County 81 over Victor Pass, the location of Bull Hill (probably unmarked, but you'll see a steel water tank and an old railroad passenger car on your right). You'll pass the site of Cameron just before the junction with the Gold Camp Road. Don't turn, but continue on County 81 to again reach Gillette. You have now encircled the mountains that were mined for gold. Turn left on Highway 67 to return to Cripple Creek.

Follow Highway 67 through Cripple Creek, but this time turn right on 2nd Street. Turn left at the next street, Carr Avenue. Carr will become County Road 1 to Florissant. The entrance to Florissant Fossil Beds National Monument will be on your left. Past the main entrance is the parking area for the Hornbeck Homestead. Continue north to the town of Florissant and the end of your journey.

Pages 212-213: This view of Cripple Creek shows why no railroad builder ever chose this route. Look on the hillside to the left of town and you will see faint lines that were once residential streets when Cripple Creek had a population of twenty-five thousand. This image was taken before legalized gambling added modern casinos to the landscape.

Crystola, now just a few commercial buildings at a wide spot in the road, had its unusual origins in the occult. Early settlers were adherents to spiritualism and psychic phenomena, popular around the time of the Civil War. In 1897, a visiting medium claimed to use his psychic power to discover gold, and investors lost all their money in a scheme than never produced an ounce of the metal.

The valley of Fountain Creek widens, and Manitou Park opens to the north. The railroad station here was first called Manitou Park and then Woodland Park. The city of Woodland Park was incorporated in 1890. Dr. William Bell (Journey 20) had already constructed a resort near here and other hotels would be built, as Woodland Park was to become the westernmost Ute Pass resort town. It was also a sawmill town with five mills turning logs into lumber. Tiny narrow-gauge trains struggled from Manitou Lake, bringing logs to the mills. Modern development has been particularly aggressive here, leaving precious few historical landmarks. You might visit the Ute Pass History Park adjacent to the Ute Pass Cultural Center (210 East Midland Avenue). The history park is operated by the Ute Pass Historical Society, whose knowledgeable volunteers can help you with the history of all the towns on Ute Pass.

The first permanent settlers in Teller County chose Divide—the summit of Ute Pass—as their new home in 1870. Soon, lumber and other commerce funneled through town. The railroad arrived in 1887 and remained until 1949. Cattlemen stopped at local false-front saloons to wet their whistles as the mournful whistle of the railroad echoed off the mountains. Not only did the waters divide here, so did the railroad tracks. The Colorado Midland continued west to Grand Junction, and the Midland Terminal turned south to Cripple Creek.

Times changed, and by the 1920s, Divide was an agricultural area with lettuce and seed potatoes shipped out on the railroad. Winter ice was harvested in Coulson Lake. Men would cut it into large blocks that were stored in insulated warehouses until they were needed to cool lettuce on its long journey to market. The railroad depot will be on your left (south) as you enter town. It has an unattractive addition that makes it hard to spot. The town's old schoolhouse is on the southwest corner of the intersection of U.S. Highway 24 and Colorado Highway 67.

Midland had a sawmill and was a water stop on the Midland Terminal Railway. After Midland, the highway is located atop the railroad grade—you can tell by the gentle grades, wide curves, huge earthen fills, deep rocky cuts, and the single-lane Waters Tunnel (renamed the Little Ike Tunnel). The road now bypasses the tunnel, but when I first arrived in Colorado, that wasn't the case.

Driving through the one-lane railroad tunnel required turning on your headlights, honking your horn, and entering slowly. The tunnel was built on a slight curve, so you had to drive partway inside before you could see if anyone had entered from the opposite direction!

There are few structures left at Gillette, where the valley opens up. The shops of the Midland Terminal were originally here, and twelve hundred people lived in what turned out to be a particularly frigid valley in a cold land. Gillette is best known for being the site of the only authentic bullfight ever held in the United States. Here, your route will diverge from that of the railway.

When Bob Womack struck gold in Poverty Gulch in 1890, the Cripple Creek & Victor Mining District was born. It was Colorado's last major historic gold rush, and peak production occurred a mere decade after first discovery. Three railroads served the five hundred mines, and two trolley lines served fifty-five thousand people in twelve towns. You'll completely circle Gold Hill—actually a substantial stand of mountains—from which the wealth was wrested from the earth. Imagine what you would have seen in 1900 with eight thousand miners working day and night, mills pounding big rocks into small rocks, trains and trolleys squealing around curves, twelve dozen saloons serving a raucous crowd, ladies of the night plying their trade, and families visiting the zoo. It must have been a remarkable sight—an urban industrial landscape two miles high!

With almost five hundred mines and three railroads, the Cripple Creek & Victor Mining District was a two-mile-high industrial labyrinth in the last years of the nineteenth century. New shafts were started. Railroad tracks were moved. Modern mining has again changed the landscape as roads are closed, opened, and relocated and whole mountaintops are moved. Maps of this area become outdated very quickly. *Denver Public Library, Western History Collection, Stewart Bros, X-62483*

As you crest a hill past Gillette, you will marvel at the spectacular aerial panorama of Cripple Creek. Perhaps you can spot the faint outlines of long-gone city streets in the now-empty fields near town. As you switchback down the steep hillside that prevented any railroad from entering from this direction, you'll come to the Mollie Kathleen Gold Mine. Take the informative tour 1,000 feet

The Cripple Creek & Victor Mining District is packed with historic sites, trails, and roads. *Southern Teller County Focus Group. In memory of Cherry Hunter. Design by ZStudios. Artwork from: Victor Lowell Thomas Museum, Teller County, Cherry Hunter, ZStudios. Copyright July 2006.*

below the earth. (The district's deepest mine was 3,500 feet.) Near the Mollie Kathleen Gold Mine is the Pikes Peak Heritage Center. Featuring aspects of a visitors' center and a media-based museum, the heritage center is a perfect place to orient yourself to the district's history.

Cripple Creek was incorporated in 1892, but a great fire destroyed it just four years later. A majestic town was built on its ashes, and by 1900, it was the largest city in the mining district and the fourth largest in Colorado. Just before you reach the historic downtown, the Cripple Creek District Museum (510 Bennett Drive) will be on your left, housed in the multistoried Midland Terminal depot. It features excellent exhibits on the railroad, mining, and Cripple Creek itself.

Fire was a deadly enemy of all Colorado's mining towns, and few escaped without at least one major conflagration. Here, horse-drawn fire equipment is parked in front of the Cripple Creek city hall and fire station. The building was constructed in 1898, two years after a great fire burned Cripple Creek to ashes. Supposedly, molten gold flowed out of the banks and into the gutters! *Colorado Historical Society, CHS.X7917*

Once, you could purchase tickets for Paris, France, in this depot—including the steamship coupon!

The very narrow-gauge steam trains of the Cripple Creek & Victor Narrow Gauge Railroad leave from the Bull Hill Depot (5 Carr Avenue), moved here from its original location east of Victor. You'll be treated to an outdoor museum of actual mines, mills, and ghost towns, all interpreted by the train's engineer.

Bennett Street bisects Cripple Creek's historic downtown, which is now filled with new gambling casinos behind the historic façades of original buildings. Brothels were once located on Myers Avenue, a block south of Bennett. One, the 1896 Old Homestead Parlor House Museum (353 Myers Avenue), has an informative tour explaining the "adult" entertainment of historic Cripple Creek.

South of Cripple Creek, you'll be on the roadbed of the narrow-gauge Florence & Cripple Creek Railroad. The first to arrive in the district in 1894, by threading its way up Phantom Canyon to the south, it was the first to be abandoned when its owners decided not to rebuild it after a 1912 flood washed away much of the track.

As you near Victor, the landscape changes dramatically because modern open-pit mining has created huge piles of tailings (waste rock) near the highway. Historic Victor is untouched and may retain its nineteenth-century ambiance better any than other major mining town in Colorado. Mine owners lived in Cripple Creek, but many of the mine workers lived in Victor. There are numerous large, historic buildings to see, and you must spend time walking around town. You can spend the night in the four-story Victor Hotel (321 Victor Avenue), beautifully restored down to its bird-cage elevator.

Sizeable buildings still spring from the mountainside at the mining town of Victor.

Scattered about the Cripple Creek & Victor Mining District, buildings with this unusual roof profile served as powder magazines where explosives were once stored. This one is on the Vindicator Valley Trail.

Adventurer and Victor native Lowell Thomas invented travelogues— motion pictures about faraway places—and toured the world presenting them. Magazine editor, radio broadcaster, the very first television newsman, and host of two television series, Thomas was a renaissance man. His hometown honors him and recalls its own history at the Victor Lowell Thomas Museum (202 Victor Avenue).

Hiking in a heavily mined area is inherently dangerous with thousand-foot-deep shafts perilously close to the surface. You will find an abundance of safe interpretive trails in the Victor area, and you should walk at least some of them. The Independence Mill Site, Battle Mountain, Golden Circle, and Vindicator Valley trails are a few of the options. All are lined with century-old mining artifacts.

The American Eagles Mine is located high above Victor, and its surface plant is open to public inspection. Most of its structures date from 1895, and at 10,570 feet above sea level it is the highest mine in the district. Then as now, the highest mine has the most breathtaking views.

The American Eagles Mine was the highest mine in the Cripple Creek & Victor Mining District. Its 1895 head frame and several buildings are open to the public.

Victor was a town for bachelor miners, full of saloons and brothels. It was Goldfield that attracted families. Drive into town and explore. The original town hall stands, as do many old residences.

You'll soon crest a hill that was the site of Bull Hill, where railroad cars were consolidated into trains for trips down to Colorado Springs. Experience a panoramic view of the west face of Pikes Peak that has no rival.

Trains leaving for Colorado Springs from Bull Hill, once a bustling railroad town, enjoyed this view of the western slopes of Pikes Peak.

Cameron was near the Gold Camp Road intersection. Here, Pinnacle Park once provided family entertainment with a zoo, carnival rides, and a picnic area. The Gold Camp Road is the route of the Colorado Springs & Cripple Creek District Railroad, known as "the Short Line" since it was the shortest track between the mining district and Colorado Springs. President Theodore Roosevelt rode the Short Line in 1901 and called it "the ride that bankrupted the English language." The track is now an unpaved road though spectacular scenery, though lack of maintenance and controversy over the road's usage

The ruins of an old railroad trestle slumber beside the Gold Camp Road. As was often the case, the railroad first built a timber trestle—quick and inexpensive to construct but expensive to maintain—and later filled the space with earth when it had more time and money. Coming full circle, the elements have slowly eroded the fill, exposing the original timbers.

requires several deviations from the railroad's original path.

On August 20, 1969, the Florissant Fossil Beds National Monument was established to protect and interpret the extensive fossils found here. Visit the small interpretive museum and hike at least some of the large trail network, which accesses areas of cultural and natural history as well as scenic beauty. Adeline Hornbek arrived here in 1878 with her children and homesteaded in this remote land. Her easily accessible cabin still stands in the national monument.

Judge James Castello, the earliest settler in this area, constructed a home and hotel in the Florissant Valley in 1870. Slowly, the town of Florissant began to take shape with a general store in 1884 and sawmills by 1887. That year also saw the town's most momentous event when the first Colorado Midland train trundled into view. People and goods moved conveniently between Florissant and Colorado Springs. Farms, ranches, and other enterprises flourished. One wonders at the level of despair in the tiny community when the railroad was closed in 1918 and dismantled in 1921. The residents were left with a dirt road for wagons and unreliable automobiles instead of a fast, comfortable train. Despair was an oft-repeated theme in Colorado after the railroads retreated and before modern automobiles and paved highways arrived. To learn more about the area's history, visit the Pikes Peak Historical Society Museum (18033 County Road 1).

Adeline Hornbek was a single mother who homesteaded in this cabin in 1887. The cabin lies within the Florissant Fossil Beds National Monument but is easily accessible through a secondary entrance.

ROYAL GORGE
Down the Arkansas

The Wet Mountain Valley is sandwiched between the Wet and the Sangre de Cristo mountains. In 1870, you would have heard settlers speaking German at the communal agricultural community of Colfax, which was founded by 357 immigrants from Germany. Though the colony failed, many of the Germans remained to farm or ranch. Other settlers would arrive, but it was the 1870 visit of General William Palmer with his friend Dr. William Bell that had the most impact on the valley. Bell was so entranced with the area that he purchased a large town site and later renamed it Westcliffe after his hometown in England. Silver mines gave birth to the neighboring town of Rosita, whose heydays lasted from 1872 to 1881, when much of the town burned to the ground. Fortunately, silver had already been discovered nearby at Silver Cliff in 1879, and five thousand people called Silver Cliff home just one year later.

Palmer's Denver & Rio Grande Railroad arrived in 1881, building its depot on Dr. Bell's land, a mile west of existing Silver Cliff. It pays to have powerful friends. Thus Westcliffe became, and still is, the predominant city in the valley. After floods washed out the narrow-gauge track along Grape Creek three times, the railroad threw in the towel in 1890. Mining ceased. Rosita became a ghost town, and Silver Cliff almost disappeared as well. Agriculture saved the valley from being abandoned, and Westcliffe became its supply center. Denver & Rio Grande trains soon arrived again—this time, standard-gauge trains whistled into town from Texas Creek until 1937, when the Great Depression silenced those mournful wails.

Drive around Westcliffe and adjacent Silver Cliff. Both harbor interesting old structures. Westcliffe has the Old School House Museum (403 South Fourth Street). The railroad's restored engine house is near the historical Railroad District's interpretive center (110 Rosita Avenue). Silver Cliff houses its museum in the Silver Cliff Town Hall and Fire Station (606 Main Street). There are also a few historic buildings still standing at Rosita.

The Royal Gorge Bridge was erected in 1929 to attract tourists, a function it has served admirably since. The rim is now populated by attractions that include a cable-car ride across the gorge and a steep incline railway that will take you down to the level of the river. The suspension bridge is 1,053 feet above the Arkansas River and is owned by Cañon City. A trolley line once connected the

The Westcliffe School House Museum dominates the foreground, with the spire of Hope Lutheran Church rising between the museum and the Sangre de Cristo Mountains.

bridge site to town. North of the Royal Gorge Bridge and Park is the Buckskin Joe Frontier Town & Railway. Here you'll find some relocated historic buildings, including the H. A. W. Tabor Store from the mining town of Buckskin Joe (Journey 8). A miniature train ride terminates at the edge of the gorge, where there is a superb view of the bridge.

After the Santa Fe's line blocked the Denver & Rio Grande's track from Raton Pass (Journey 18), the two railroads again battled for a route, this time in the bottom of the 1,000-foot-deep Royal Gorge—only 30 feet wide at its narrowest point. This time the battle was fought with real bullets and famous gunslingers, like Bat Masterson. The war ended in a stalemate, and a treaty enabled the Denver & Rio Grande to build through the gorge. Ride a passenger train of the Royal Gorge Route Railroad through the deepest, narrowest slit in the mountains under the Royal Gorge Bridge. Trains depart from the historic Santa Fe depot (401 Water Street) in Cañon City.

DIRECTIONS

Start your journey by exploring Silver Cliff on Colorado Highway 96 west of Pueblo. Drive west on Highway 96, Main Street, to Westcliffe.

> **OPTIONAL:** *To experience Rosita, go south on 6th Street, Colorado Highway 69. Turn left on Rosita Road, County Road 328, to reach Rosita. Return the way you came.*

Go west on Main Street and then north on 3rd Street to stay on Highway 69. At Texas Creek, turn right on U.S. Highway 50. A right turn on County Road 3A will take you to Buckskin Joe Frontier Town & Railway and the Royal Gorge Bridge and Park. Return the way you came and turn right on U.S. 50 for Cañon City. At the west end of town, Cañon City's historic downtown stretches along Main Street, parallel to and north of U.S. 50 (Royal Gorge Boulevard). The Royal Gorge Route Railroad's depot is reached by going south on 3rd Street. Visit the Abbey on U.S. 50 on the east side of town.

Drive south on 9th Street and follow Colorado Highway 115 signs to reach Florence. Proceed north on Pikes Peak Avenue, Colorado Highway 67.

> **OPTIONAL:** *Cross U.S. 50 (at a stoplight) to experience the unpaved Phantom Canyon Road. End your excursion in Victor and return the way you came.*

Travel east on U.S. 50 to Pueblo. A Pueblo city map will be essential to navigating in town.

The Royal Gorge Bridge is the highest suspension bridge in the world. The railroad track below it was originally built by the Santa Fe, but possession of the railroad right-of-way was challenged in the "Royal Gorge War." During the dispute, bullets were actually fired by gunfighters, including the legendary Bat Masterson. Terms of the "peace treaty" included the ceding of the route to the Denver & Rio Grande.

Cañon City was founded in 1860 as a supply center for mining and agriculture. The Museum of Colorado Prisons (201 North 1st Street) is housed in the original 1935 Women's Correctional Facility. The first inmate arrived at Cañon City's first prison, the Colorado Territorial Prison, in 1871. The Royal Gorge Regional Museum and History Center is located in the 1927 Municipal Building (612 Royal Gorge Boulevard). The building is on the National Register of Historic Places, as is the old downtown of about eighty buildings. The Benedictine Holy Cross Abbey was established in 1926. Along with having been a monastery, it has had other uses, including that of school. Today, no longer owned by the Benedictines, The Abbey (2951 East US Highway 50), hosts The Winery at Holy Cross Abbey (3011 East US Highway 50), as well as serving several other new functions. It is a beautiful historic site worth visiting.

The second commercial oil field in the United States was discovered near Florence in 1862. Florence became a major center of the nascent petroleum industry as the twentieth century dawned. In 1892, Cañon City built the Shelf Road, then a toll road, to the Cripple Creek & Victor Mining District. To ensure its share of the riches, Florence constructed the Florence and Cripple Creek *Free* Road through Phantom Canyon. Florence won the major portion of trade with the Cripple Creek & Victor Mining District when the Florence & Cripple Creek Railroad was built on the grade of its free road in 1894. Smelters were built near Florence to process ore from the Cripple Creek & Victor Mining District (Journey 21). The Florence & Cripple Creek Railroad was washed out by a 1912 flood, never to be rebuilt, and the right-of-way became the Phantom Canyon Road, now a historic byway to and from Victor. There are two railroad tunnels, an original steel bridge, and the remnants of a few structures along the way.

The Phantom Canyon Road was once the route of the narrow-gauge Florence & Cripple Creek Railroad, which bored this tunnel through solid rock. Automobile traffic is obviously limited to one direction at a time.

The Royal Gorge Route operates vintage streamlined passenger trains through the Royal Gorge, including elegant dinner trains.

Still later, coal was discovered and mined south of Florence. Short railroads were built to carry coal to a connection with the Denver & Rio Grande Railroad. It is no wonder that downtown Florence is populated with large buildings of brick and stone, for prosperity arrived in three forms: oil, gold, and coal. Don't forget to stop at the Price Pioneer Museum (100 East Front Street).

A small trading community grew near the junction of Fountain Creek and the Arkansas River. Here, the adobe buildings of El Pueblo were constructed in 1842. Pueblo was incorporated in 1870, but the origin of the modern city began in 1886, when the cities of South Pueblo and Central Pueblo merged with Pueblo. In 1894, the town of Bessemer was melted into the mix.

General William Palmer needed steel rails for his expanding railroad empire, and manufacturing them locally in his own plant was clearly advantageous. Three predecessor companies were amalgamated into the Colorado Coal & Iron

The magnificent Rosemount Museum in Pueblo is the most spectacular preserved home in Colorado.

Company in 1880. In 1892, CC&I was merged into John Osgood's competing Colorado Fuel Company, creating the Colorado Fuel & Iron Company. CF&I was the first vertically integrated steel mill in the American West, meaning that it controlled the entire production process from the mining of raw materials through the production of steel to the manufacture of railroad rail. The company controlled about five dozen mines, including coal mines near Redstone (Journey 2) and Trinidad (Journey 18); an iron mine north of Salida (Journey 11); and a limestone quarry on Monarch Pass (Journey 11). Mines were located in other states as well.

In 1903, a cash shortage put the mill in the hands of John D. Rockefeller. With thousands of employees, CF&I was the state's largest employer for many years. It was a pioneer in labor relations, both good and bad. Despite efforts at modernization, CF&I declared bankruptcy in 1990 as a result of foreign competition. The facilities are operated today on a much smaller scale as the Rocky Mountain Steel Mill, which is owned by Evraz Oregon Steel Mills. The Steelworks Museum of Industry and Culture (215-225 Canal Street) does a superb job of interpreting its namesake story, so central to Pueblo's history. The museum is housed in the CF&I Dispensary Building and will eventually move to the adjacent 1901 CF&I headquarters building. Pueblo always reminds me of a mini-sized Chicago, the city where I grew up, with heavy industry, colorful commercial districts, ethnic restaurants, a strong sense of community, and large railroad yards. It is a less crowded Chicago, but with a view of the mountains!

Businessman John Thatcher and his wife, Margaret, completed a thirty-seven-room home at Pueblo in 1893. Owned by the same family until the 1960s, the grand building's furnishings are nearly all original. The mansion—the most spectacular preserved home in Colorado—is now the Rosemount Museum (419 West 14th Street), and the adjacent carriage house is now a restaurant. The site of the original El Pueblo trading post is an archaeological excavation operated by the Colorado Historical Society as part of the El Pueblo Museum (301 North Union) on the north end of the Union Avenue Historic District. Denver & Rio Grande trains no longer depart from the old freight depot, which has become the Southeast Colorado Heritage Center (201 West B Street) near the south end of the historic district. Don't miss the Pueblo Railway Museum across the street from the heritage center. Walk through the historic district and enjoy the many old buildings, including the beautifully restored Pueblo Union Depot (132 West B Street).

Restored Mine Rescue Car No. 1 rests outside Pueblo's Steelworks Museum of Industry and Culture. The car rushed rescue equipment to the scene of mine disasters at the numerous coal mines along the Colorado & Wyoming Railway west of Trinidad.

ACKNOWLEDGMENTS

I would especially like to thank my wife, Margaret, for her help, patience, and love over decades of my infatuation with Colorado's history. Our children, Kevin and Karen, were the most pleasant companions on excursions—when they weren't fighting in the back seat. As adults, they still sometimes join us on trips into the mountains, but fortunately, they no longer fight. I am especially grateful to Kevin, who contributed his time and talent to the creation of this book.

I'd also like to thank the people and organizations who helped provide specific information for this book, including Donald Tallman and Charles Albi of the Colorado Railroad Museum; Betty Kilsdonk of the Estes Park Museum; Patti Markle of the Mancos Valley Visitor Center; Clarke Becker, President/ CEO of the Colorado Rural Development Council; Rev. Walther A. Olsen of the First Baptist Church of Dolores; the Cañon City Chamber of Commerce; Paula Sheagley of The Abbey in Cañon City; Anna Orgeron of the Custer County Merchants & Chamber of Commerce; Jason Midyette, formerly of the Colorado Time Table; Ruth Zirkle-Zalewski of the Southern Teller County Focus Group; Don Shank of the Denver & Rio Grande Historical Foundation and the Denver & Rio Grande Railroad; Bob Shank of the Rio Grande Scenic Railroad; Wendy Roberts of the Rangely Arts Council; Vanessa Huber of the Rangely Chamber of Commerce; Jim Wetzel of the Delta County Museum; Ann Honchell of the New Castle Library; Mickey Tucker of the New Castle Chamber of Commerce; Linda Lysaght of the Ridgway Area Chamber of Commerce; Freda Peterson of the San Juan County Historical Society; Chuck Fairchild of the Creede Underground Mining Museum; Sue Fouse of the Bent County Development Foundation; Brittany Stevenson of Van Briggle Pottery; Pete Davis of Giuseppe's Old Depot Restaurant; the U. S. Air Force Academy Public Affairs Office; the Victor Lowell Thomas Museum; the Victor Hotel; Martha Owens of the Creede-Mineral County Chamber of Commerce; the Evans Chamber of Commerce; Don Cook of the Mountain Bike Hall of Fame; Angela of Rebeltec; and Sue Griswold of the Greater Woodland Park Chamber of Commerce.

BIBLIOGRAPHY

Colorado Atlas & Gazetteer. 4th ed. Yarmouth, Maine: DeLorme, 1998.
> This is a single convenient volume of topographic maps of the entire state. You may find it difficult to read if you are unfamiliar with topographic maps, but there is no single source of more detailed maps.

Danilov, Victor J. *Colorado Museums and Historic Sites*. Boulder, Colorado: University of Colorado Press, 2000.
> This catalog-like publication includes all museums throughout the state, not just those related to Colorado's history. There is a brief description of each.

Massey, Peter, and Jeanne Wilson. *4WD Adventures Colorado*. Castle Rock, Colorado: Swagman Publishing, Inc., 1998.
> This guide has easy-to-understand maps, rates roads by difficulty, and includes virtually every interesting destination for which you might need a four-wheel-drive vehicle. Its extensive introductory section includes topics that range from driving difficult roads to the identification of wildflowers. GPS coordinates are included.

Murray, Robert B., and Russell D. Lee. *Colorado Ghost Town and Mining Camp Guide*. Commerce City, Colorado: Colorado Recreation Guides, 1976.
> This out-of-print atlas is unattractive and difficult to understand. However, it is your last resort when no other reference lists some obscure place. You might try to find it in a library if you cannot find a location in more available sources.

Ormes, Robert M. *Tracking Ghost Railroads in Colorado*. Colorado Springs, Colorado: Green Light Graphics, 1992.
> This out-of-print guidebook is the only comprehensive atlas of thousands of miles of abandoned railroad grades. It includes brief histories of locations and the railroads that ran there. Popular with hikers and cross-country skiers as well as railroad and history enthusiasts, it was reprinted ten times. You may want to search for a used copy.

Varney, Philip, and John Drew. *Ghost Towns of Colorado*. Stillwater, Minnesota: Voyageur Press, 1999.
> This attractive pictorial history describes Colorado's most popular ghost towns and includes easy-to-follow maps.

Wiatrowski, Claude. *Railroads of Colorado*. Stillwater, Minnesota: Voyageur Press, 2002.
> This comprehensive history of Colorado's railroads is illustrated with many attractive photographs. An excellent color-coded map of Colorado's complex historic railroad network is included. No other single volume will introduce you to all the state's railroad history.

APPENDIX
Useful Websites

Map Sources

U.S. Geological Survey (paper maps, electronic data)	http://www.usgs.gov/pubprod/
Google Maps (online street maps, many backroads)	http://maps.google.com/
MapQuest (online street maps, many backroads)	http://www.mapquest.com/
Trails.com (online USGS topographic maps)	http://www.trails.com/
Mytopo.com (customized paper topographic maps)	http://www.mytopo.com/
U.S. Forest Service (online maps)	http://www.fs.fed.us/r2/maps/
U.S. Forest Service (paper maps)	http://www.nationalforeststore.com/

Chapter 1
Journey 1

Fruita	http://www.fruitachamber.org/
Dinosaur Journey Museum	http://www.dinosaurjourney.org/
Colorado National Monument	http://www.nps.gov/colm/
Grand Junction	http://www.gjchamber.org/
Downtown Grand Junction	http://www.downtowngj.org/
Cross Orchards Historic Site	http://www.wcmuseum.org/crossorchards.htm
Mesa State College	http://www.mesastate.edu/
Avalon Theatre	http://www.avalontheatregj.com/
Museum of the West	http://www.wcmuseum.org/
Palisade	http://www.palisadecoc.com/
Grand Mesa	http://www.grandmesabyway.org/
Delta	http://www.deltacolorado.org/
Delta County Museum	http://deltacountymuseum.org/
Delta United Methodist Church	
(Historic First Methodist Episcopal)	http://www.deltaumc.org/
Delta Municipal Light & Power Plant	http://www.delta-co.gov/ cityDepts_utilities_history.htm
Orchard City	http://www.orchardcityco.org/
Cedaredge	http://www.cedaredgecolorado.com/
Pioneer Town	http://www.pioneertown.org/

Journey 2

Marble	http://www.marbletourismassociation.org/
Redstone	http://www.redstonecolorado.com/
Redstone Inn	http://www.redstoneinn.com/
Redstone Castle (Historic Cleveholm Manor)	http://www.redstonecastle.us/
Carbondale	http://www.carbondale.com/
Mount Sopris Historical Museum	http://www.mtsoprishistoricalsociety.org/
Basalt	http://www.basaltchamber.org/
Aspen	http://www.aspenchamber.org/
Ashcroft	http://www.aspenhistorysociety.com/ ashcroftmuseum
Wheeler Opera House	http://www.wheeleroperahouse.com/
Hotel Jerome	http://hoteljerome.rockresorts.com/
Wheeler/Stallard Museum	http://www.aspenhistorysociety.com/ wheelermuseum

Journey 3

New Castle	http://www.newcastlechamber.org/Chamber.htm
New Castle Historical Museum	http://www.newcastlecolorado.com/history/ museum.htm
Rifle	http://www.riflechamber.com/
Meeker	http://www.meekerchamber.com/
White River Museum	http://www.meekercolorado.com/museum.htm
Rangely	http://www.rangelychamber.com/
Rangely Outdoor Museum	http://www.rangely.com/Museum.htm
Dinosaur National Monument	http://www.nps.gov/dino/

Journey 4

Craig	http://www.craig-chamber.com/
Museum of Northwest Colorado	http://www.museumnwco.org/
Steamboat Springs	http://www.steamboat-chamber.com/
Tread of Pioneers Museum	http://www.yampavalley.info/treadofpioneers.asp
The Eleanor Bliss Center for the Arts at the Depot	http://www.steamboatspringsarts.com/
Glenwood Springs	http://www.glenwoodchamber.com/
Glenwood Railroad Museum	http://www.glenwoodrailroadmuseum.org/
Hotel Colorado	http://www.hotelcolorado.com/

Frontier Historical Museum	http://glenwoodhistory.com/
Glenwood Caverns Adventure Park	http://www.glenwoodcaverns.com/

Chapter 2

Journey 5

Hot Sulphur Springs Resort	http://www.hotsulphursprings.com/
Grand County Historical Association Pioneer Village	http://www.grandcountymuseum.com/
Kremmling	http://www.kremmlingchamber.com/
Granby	http://www.granbychamber.com/
Grand Lake	http://www.grandlakechamber.com/
Kaufmann House Museum	http://www.kauffmanhouse.org/
Estes Park	http://www.estesparkresort.com/
Rocky Mountain National Park	http://www.nps.gov/romo/
Enos Mills Cabin	http://home.earthlink.net/~enosmillscbn/
Stanley Hotel	http://www.stanleyhotel.com/
Fall River Hydro Plant	http://www.estesnet.com/LightPower/ hydro_plant.aspx
Estes Park Museum	http://www.estesnet.com/Museum/
Lula W. Dorsey Museum, YMCA Camp of the Rockies	http://www.ymcarockiesmuseum.org/
MacGregor Ranch Museum	http://www.macgregorranch.org/
Loveland	http://www.loveland.org/
Loveland Museum/Gallery	http://www.ci.loveland.co.us/ Cultural_Services/cultural_services_museum.htm

Journey 6

Fort Collins	http://www.fcchamber.org/
Old Town (online walking tour brochure)	http://www.downtownfortcollins.com/
Colorado State University	http://www.colostate.edu/
Fort Collins Municipal Railway (streetcars)	http://www.fortnet.org/trolley/
Avery House	http://www.poudrelandmarks.com/ plf_avery_house.shtml
Fort Collins Waterworks	http://www.poudrelandmarks.com/ plf_water_works.shtml
Museo de las Tres Colonias (Romero House)	http://www.poudrelandmarks.com/plf_museo.shtml
Fort Collins Museum	http://www.ci.fort-collins.co.us/museum/

Greeley   http://www.greeleychamber.com/

    Centennial Village Museum   http://www.greeleygov.com/museums/
          CentennialVillage.aspx

    Greeley History Museum   http://www.greeleygov.com/museums/
          GreeleyHistoryMuseum.aspx

    Meeker Museum   http://www.greeleygov.com/museums/
          MeekerHome.aspx

Evans   http://www.evanschamber.org/

    Fort Vasquez Museum   http://www.coloradohistory.org/hist_sites/
          ft_vasquez/ft_vasquez.htm

Longmont   http://www.longmontchamber.org/

    Longmont St. Vrain Historical Society   http://www.stvrainhistoricalsociety.org/
    Longmont Museum   http://www.ci.longmont.co.us/museum/

Lyons   http://www.lyons-colorado.com/

    Lyons Redstone Museum   http://www.townoflyons.com/about_lyons.html

Boulder   http://www.boulderchamber.com/

    University of Colorado   http://www.colorado.edu/
    University of Colorado Heritage Center   http://cuheritage.org/
    Downtown Boulder   http://www.boulderdowntown.com/
    Historic Boulder   http://www.historicboulder.org/
    Boulder History Museum   http://www.boulderhistorymuseum.org/
    Harbeck-Bergheim House   http://www.boulderhistorymuseum.org/harbeck.asp
    Colorado Chautauqua National Historic Landmark   http://www.chautauqua.com/
    Hotel Boulderado   http://www.boulderado.com/
    Boulder Theatre   http://www.bouldertheater.com/

Journey 7

Englewood   http://www.englewoodchamber.org/

Denver   http://www.denverchamber.org/

    Confluence Park   http://www.denvergov.org/tabid/393910/
          Default.aspx

    REI Store   http://www.rei.com/stores/denverflagship/
    Larimer Square Historic District   http://www.larimersquare.com/
    Colorado History Museum   http://www.coloradohistory.org/hist_sites/
          CHM/Colorado_History_Museum.htm

    Paramount Theatre   http://www.denverparamount.com/

Brown Palace Hotel	http://www.brownpalace.com/
Trinity United Methodist Church	http://www.trinityumc.org/
Governor's Residence at the Boettcher Mansion	http://www.colorado.gov/governor/residence/
Colorado State Capitol Building	http://www.state.co.us/gov_dir/leg_dir/lcsstaff/ Scrollpages/TourScroll.htm
Molly Brown House	http://mollybrown.org/
Black American West Museum	http://www.blackamericanwestmuseum.com/
Denver Firefighters Museum	http://www.denverfirefightersmuseum.org/
Four Mile Historic Park	http://www.fourmilepark.org/
Byers-Evans House	http://www.coloradohistory.org/hist_sites/ Byers_Evans/byers_evans.htm
Littleton Historical Museum	http://www.littletongov.org/museum/
Aurora History Museum	http://www.ci.aurora.co.us/AuroraGov/Departments/ Library__Recreation_and_Cultural_Services/ Cultural_Services/History_Museum/
Golden	http://www.goldencochamber.org/
Colorado Railroad Museum	http://www.crrm.org/
Adolph Coors Company	http://www.coors.com/
Colorado School of Mines	http://www.mines.edu/
Golden Pioneer Museum	http://www.goldenpioneermuseum.com/
Central City	http://www.centralcitycolorado.us/
Central City Opera House	http://www.centralcityopera.org/ index.cgi?CONTENT_ID=156
Gilpin History Museum	http://www.gilpinhistory.org/ gilpin_history_museum.html
Blackhawk	http://www.cityofblackhawk.org/
Idaho Springs, Georgetown, Silver Plume	http://www.clearcreekcounty.org/
Idaho Springs	http://idahospringschamber.org/
Argo Gold Mine and Mill	http://www.historicargotours.com/
Underhill Museum	http://www.historicidahosprings.com/ attractions/underhill_museum.php
Heritage Museum	http://www.historicidahosprings.com/ attractions/heritage_museum.php
Georgetown	http://www.visitgeorgetowncolorado.com/
Georgetown Gateway Visitors Center	http://www.historicgeorgetown.org/ properties/visitorcenter.htm

Hamill House	http://www.historicgeorgetown.org/houses/hamill.htm
Hotel de Paris Museum	http://www.hoteldeparismuseum.org/
Georgetown Energy Museum	http://georgetownenergymuseum.org/
Georgetown-Silver Plume Historic District	http://tps.cr.nps.gov/nhl/detail.cfm?ResourceId=147&ResourceType=District
Georgetown Loop Historic Mining and Railroad Park	http://www.coloradohistory.org/hist_sites/Georgetown/G_loop.htm
Georgetown Loop Railroad	http://georgetownlooprr.com/
Silver Plume	http://www.townofsilverplume.org/
Silver Plume George Rowe Museum	http://www.coloradostylepublishing.com/rowemuseum.html

Journey 8

Morrison Historic District	http://historicmorrison.org/history/
Morrison Heritage Museum	http://historicmorrison.org/history/mhm.php
Dinosaur Ridge	http://www.dinoridge.org/
Bailey	http://www.baileycolorado.org/
Como	http://www.southparkchamber.com/
Boreas Pass	http://www.fs.fed.us/r2/psicc/sopa/boreas.shtml
Robert's Cabin	http://www.fs.fed.us/r2/psicc/sopa/roberts.shtml
Baker Tank	http://www.summithistorical.org/BakerTank.html
Summit County (Breckenridge)	http://summitchamber.org/
Breckenridge	http://www.gobreck.com/
Rotary Snow Plow Park	http://www.summithistorical.org/RailwayRotary.html
Alice G. Milne House	http://www.summithistorical.org/MilneHouse.html
National Historic District of Breckenridge	http://www.summithistorical.org/breckhistoricdist.htm
Edwin Carter Museum	http://www.summithistorical.org/Edwin.html
Breckenridge Heritage Alliance (many tours)	http://www.breckheritage.com/
Washington Mine	http://www.summithistorical.org/Washington.html

Lomax Placer Gulch	http://www.summithistorical.org/Lomax.html
Country Boy Mine	http://www.countryboymine.com/
Father Dyer Cabin	http://www.summithistorical.org/FatherDyerCabin.html
Fairplay, Alma	http://www.southparkchamber.com/
South Park City	http://www.southparkcity.org/

Journey 9

Northeast Colorado Tourism	http://www.northeastcoloradotourism.com/
Overland Trail	http://www.over-land.com/
Fort Morgan	http://www.fortmorganchamber.org/
Fort Morgan Museum	http://www.ftmorganmus.org/
Glenn Miller Orchestra	http://www.fortmorganchamber.org/default.php
Sterling	http://www.logancountychamber.com/index.htm
Overland Trail Museum	http://www.sterlingcolo.com/pages/dept/plr/museum.php
Sedgwick County (Julesburg, Ovid)	http://www.sedgwickcountyco.com/
Ovid	http://www.clintoncountychamber.org/ovid.php
Julesburg	http://www.townofjulesburg.com/
Fort Sedgwick Museum, Depot Museum	http://users.kci.net/history/

Chapter 3

Journey 10

Minturn	http://www.minturn.org/
Camp Hale	http://www.mscd.edu/~history/camphale/index.html
Camp Hale Military Munitions Project	http://www.camphale.org/
National Association of the Tenth Mountain Division	http://www.10thmtndivassoc.org/
Leadville	http://www.visitleadvilleco.com/
Matchless Mine	http://matchlessmine.com/
Tabor Opera House	http://www.taboroperahouse.net/
National Mining Hall of Fame and Museum	http://www.mininghalloffame.org/
Healy House and Dexter Cabin Museum	http://www.coloradohistory.org/hist_sites/healyhouse/h_house.htm
Leadville Colorado & Southern Railroad	http://www.leadville-train.com/

Twin Lakes	http://www.visitleadvilleco.com/
Inter-Laken Hotel	http://www.usbr.gov/gp/archive/glimpse/ interlaken.cfm
Twin Lakes Village (Dayton)	http://twinlakesco.com/
Buena Vista	http://www.buenavistacolorado.org/
Buena Vista Heritage Museum	http://www.buenavistaheritage.org/

Journey 11

Salida	http://www.salidachamber.org/
Salida Museum	http://www.salidachamber.org/museum/
Pitkin	http://www.pitkincolorado.com/
Alpine Tunnel Historic District	http://www.narrowgauge.org/alpine-tunnel/html/
Gunnison	http://www.gunnison-co.com/
Gunnison - Crested Butte Tourism Association	http://www.gunnisoncrestedbutte.com/
Western State College	http://www.western.edu/
Gunnison Pioneer Museum	http://www.PioneerTrainMuseum.org
Crested Butte	http://www.cbchamber.com/
Mountain Bike Hall of Fame	http://www.mtnbikehalloffame.com/
Rocky Mountain Biological Laboratory (Gothic)	http://rmbl.org/

Journey 12

Curecanti National Recreation Area	http://www.nps.gov/cure/
Cimarron National Park Service Visitor's Center	http://www.nps.gov/cure/historyculture/ cimarron.htm
Black Canyon of the Gunnison National Park	http://www.nps.gov/blca/
Montrose	http://www.visitmontrose.net/
Montrose County Historical Museum	http://www.visitmontrose.net/museum.htm
Ute Indian Museum and Ouray Memorial Park	http://www.coloradohistory.org/hist_sites/ uteindian/ute_Indian.htm

Chapter 4
Journey 13

Mesa Verde National Park	http://www.nps.gov/meve/
Mesa Verde Area Tourist Information	http://www.mesaverdecountry.com/
Canyon of the Ancients National Monument	http://www.blm.gov/co/st/en/nm/canm.html

Lowry Pueblo	http://www.blm.gov/co/st/en/fo/ahc/
	archaeological_sites/lowry_pueblo.html
Anasazi Heritage Center	http://www.blm.gov/co/st/en/fo/ahc.html
Hovenweep National Monument	http://www.nps.gov/hove/
Ute Mountain Ute Tribe	http://www.utemountainute.com/
Cortez	http://www.cortezchamber.com/
Cortez Cultural Center	http://www.cortezculturalcenter.org/
Crow Canyon Archaeological Site	http://www.crowcanyon.org/

Journey 14

Mancos	http://www.mancosvalley.com/
Dolores	http://www.doloreschamber.com/
McPhee Reservoir	http://www.doloreswater.com/
Rio Grande Southern Museum	
& the Dolores Visitors Center	http://doloresgallopinggoose5.com/
Rico	http://www.ricocolorado.org/
Ames Power Plant	http://www.old-engine.com/ames.htm
Illium	http://www.campilium.com/history.html
Telluride	http://www.telluridechamber.com/
New Sheridan Hotel	http://www.newsheridan.com/
Telluride Historical Museum	http://www.telluridemuseum.org/
Ridgway	http://ridgwaycolorado.com/
Ridgway Railroad Museum	http://www.ridgwayrailroadmuseum.org/

Journey 15

Ouray	http://www.ouraycolorado.com/
Ouray County Museum	http://www.ouraycountyhistoricalsociety.org/
Bachelor-Syracuse Mine	http://www.bachelorsyracusemine.com/
Silverton	http://www.silvertoncolorado.com/
Durango & Silverton Narrow Gauge Railroad	http://www.durangotrain.com/
Grand Imperial Hotel	http://www.grandimperialhotel.com/
San Juan County Historical Society Museum	http://www.silvertonhistoricsociety.org/
	index_files/page0012.htm
Mayflower Mill	http://www.silvertonhistoricsociety.org/
	index_files/page0017.htm
Old Hundred Gold Mine	http://www.minetour.com/

Durango	http://www.durango.org/
Strater Hotel	http://www.strater.com/
Animas Museum	http://www.animasmuseum.org/
Fort Lewis College	http://explore.fortlewis.edu/
Southern Ute Indian Tribe	http://www.southern-ute.nsn.us/
Chimney Rock Archaeological Area	http://www.chimneyrockco.org/
Jicarilla Apache Nation	http://jicarillaonline.com/
Pagosa Springs	http://visitpagosasprings.com/
San Juan Historical Society History Museum	http://www.pagosamuseum.org/

Chapter 5
Journey 16

Chama, New Mexico	http://www.chamavalley.com/
Friends of the Cumbres & Toltec Scenic Railroad	http://www.cumbrestoltec.org/
Antonito	http://www.slvguide.com/Antonito/ chamberofcommerce.htm
Cumbres & Toltec Scenic Railroads	http://www.cumbrestoltec.com/
Conejos (County Tourism)	http://www.conejosvacation.com/
Our Lady of Guadalupe Church	http://www.dioceseofpueblo.com/parishes/ City/bcconejos.htm
Jack Dempsey Museum and Park (Manassa)	http://www.museumtrail.org/ JackDempseyMuseum.asp
San Luis	http://sangres.com/colorado/costilla/sanluis.htm
Sangre de Cristo Church	http://www.dioceseofpueblo.com/parishes/ City/bcsanluis2.htm#San%20Luis%20History
Shrine of the Stations of the Cross	http://www.costilla-county.com/ stationsofthecross.html
San Luis Museum	http://www.museumtrail.org/SanLuisMuseum.asp
Fort Garland Museum	http://www.coloradohistory.org/hist_sites/ ft_Garland/ft_garland.htm
Great Sand Dunes National Park & Preserve	http://www.nps.gov/grsa/
San Luis Valley	http://www.slvguide.com/
Alamosa	http://www.alamosa.org/
Adams State College	http://www.adams.edu/
San Luis Valley Museum	http://www.museumtrail.org/ SanLuisValleyHistoryMuseum.asp

Rio Grande Scenic Railroad   http://riograndescenicrailroad.com/

Journey 17

South Fork   http://www.southfork.org/

Creede   http://www.creede.com/

     Creede Historical Museum & Research Library   http://www.museumtrail.org/
creedehistoricmuseum.asp

     Creede Underground Mining Museum   http://www.museumtrail.org/
CreedeUndergroundMiningMuseum.asp

     Bachelor   http://www.creede.com/bachelor_loop.htm

Lake City   http://www.lakecity.com/

     Hinsdale County Museum   http://www.lakecitymuseum.com/

     Hard Tack Mine   http://hardtack81235.tripod.com/

Journey 18

Walsenburg   http://www.huerfanocountychamberofcommerce.com/

     Walsenburg Mining Museum   http://huerfanomuseums.org/Walsenburg%20
Mining%20Museum.html

La Veta   http://www.lavetacucharachamber.com/

     Francisco Fort Museum   http://huerfanomuseums.org/Francisco%20Fort%20
Museum%20in%20La%20Veta%20Colorado.html

Stonewall   http://www.trinidadco.com/Main/Stonewall.asp

Trinidad   http://www.trinidadchamber.com/

     Trinidad History Museum   http://www.coloradohistory.org/hist_sites/
trinidad/trinidad.htm

     Trinidad State Junior College   http://www.trinidadstate.edu/

Ludlow   http://www.santafetrailscenicandhistoricbyway.org/
ludlow.html

Chapter 6

Journey 19

Rocky Ford   http://rockyfordchamber.net/

     Rocky Ford Museum   http://www.rockyfordmuseum.com/

La Junta   http://www.lajuntachamber.com/

     Koshare Indian Museum   http://www.kosharehistory.org/

Otero Museum	http://www.coloradoplains.com/otero/museum/
Bent's Old Fort National Historic Site	http://www.nps.gov/beol/
Las Animas	http://www.bentcounty.org/
Kit Carson Museum, Boggsville	http://www.phsbc.info/
Santa Fe National Historic Trail	http://www.nps.gov/safe/
Santa Fe Trail Association	http://www.santafetrail.org/
Santa Fe Trail Mountain Branch	http://www.santafetrailscenicandhistoricbyway.org/
Fort Lyon National Cemetery	http://www.cem.va.gov/CEM/cems/nchp/ftlyon.asp
Lamar	http://www.lamarchamber.com/
Big Timbers Museum	http://www.bigtimbers.org/
Camp Amache	http://www.santafetrailscenicandhistoricbyway.org/amache.html
Sand Creek Massacre National Historic Site	http://www.nps.gov/sand/
Eads	http://www.kiowacountycolo.com/eadsframe.htm
Kiowa County Historical Museum	http://www.kiowacountycolo.com/museum.htm
Kit Carson	http://www.kitcarsoncolorado.com/
Kit Carson Museum	http://www.ourjourney.info/MyJourneyDestinations/KitCarsonMuseum.asp
Cheyenne Wells	http://www.townofcheyennewells.com/
Cheyenne County Museum	http://www.ourjourney.info/MyJourneyDestinations/CheyenneCountyMuseum.asp
Burlington	http://www.burlingtoncolo.com/visitorinformation.html
Old Town Museum	http://www.burlingtoncolo.com/oldtown.html
Kit Carson County Carousel	http://www.kitcarsoncountycarousel.com/
Limon	http://www.limonchamber.com/
Limon Heritage Museum and Railroad Park	http://www.townoflimon.com/index.php?option=com_content&task=blogcategory&id=13&Itemid=48

Journey 20

Pikes Peak Country Attractions Association	http://www.pikes-peak.com/
Colorado Springs	http://www.experiencecoloradosprings.com/
Antlers Hilton Hotel	http://www.antlers.com/
Giuseppe's Old Depot Restaurant	http://www.giuseppes-depot.com/

McAllister House	http://www.nscda.org/co/ mcallisterhousemuseum.html
Colorado Springs Pioneers Museum	http://www.cspm.org/
Colorado Springs & Interurban Railway	http://www.coloradospringstrolleys.com/
Broadmoor Hotel	http://www.rockledgeranch.com/
Cheyenne Mountain Zoo	http://www.cmzoo.org/
ProRodeo Hall of Fame and Museum of the American Cowboy	http://www.prorodeohalloffame.com/
United States Air Force Academy	http://www.usafa.af.mil/
Western Museum of Mining and Industry	http://www.wmmi.org/
Old Colorado City	http://www.shopoldcoloradocity.com/
Van Briggle Pottery	http://www.vanbriggle.com/
Ghost Town Museum	http://www.ghosttownmuseum.com/
Old Colorado City History Center	http://history.oldcolo.com/
Garden of the Gods	http://www.gardenofgods.com/
Rock Ledge Ranch	http://www.rockledgeranch.com/
Manitou Springs	http://www.manitousprings.org/
Briarhurst Manor Restaurant	http://www.briarhurst.com/
Cliff House	http://www.thecliffhouse.com/
Cave of the Winds	http://www.caveofthewinds.com/
Manitou & Pike's Peak Railway	http://www.cograilway.com/
Cliff Dwellings Museum	http://www.cliffdwellingsmuseum.com/
Miramont Castle Museum	http://www.miramontcastle.org/

Journey 21

Church of the Wildwood (Green Mountain Falls)	http://www.wildwoodchurchgmf.org/
Woodland Park	http://www.woodlandparkchamber.com/
Pikes Peak Mini-Museum and the Ute Pass History Park	http://www.utepasshistoricalsociety.org/
Ute Pass Cultural Center	http://www.utepassculturalcenter.itgo.com/
Cripple Creek	http://www.visitcripplecreek.com/
Mollie Kathleen Gold Mine	http://www.goldminetours.com/
Pikes Peak Heritage Center	http://www.cripple-creek.co.us/ PikesPeakHeritageCenter.aspx
Cripple Creek District Museum	http://www.cripple-creek.org/
Cripple Creek & Victor Narrow Gauge Railroad	http://www.cripplecreekrailroad.com/
Old Homestead Parlor House Museum	http://www.cripple-creek.org/Old_Homestead/ homestead_house.html

Victor   http://www.victorcolorado.com/

    Victor Hotel   http://victorhotelcolorado.com/

    Victor Lowell Thomas Museum   http://www.victorcolorado.com/museum.htm

    Vindicator Valley and other trails   http://www.victorcolorado.com/hiking.htm

    American Eagles Mine   http://www.victorcolorado.com/eagles.htm

Florissant   http://montesanoenterprises.com/florissantco.htm

    Florissant Fossil Beds National Monument   http://www.nps.gov/flfo/

    Pikes Peak Historical Society Museum http://www.pikespeakhsmuseum.org/

Journey 22

Westcliffe   http://www.custercountyco.com/

    Old School House Museum   http://www.custercountyco.com/museums.htm

    Railroad District Interpretive Center http://www.allaboardwestcliffe.com/

Silver Cliff   http://silvercliffco.com/

Cañon City   http://www.canoncity.com/

    Royal Gorge Bridge and Park   http://www.royalgorgebridge.com/

    Buckskin Joe Frontier Town & Railway http://www.buckskinjoe.com/Default.asp

    Royal Gorge Route Railroad   http://www.royalgorgeroute.com/

    Museum of Colorado Prisons   http://www.prisonmuseum.org/

    Royal Gorge Regional Museum and History Center   http://www.royalgorgehistory.org/
RGRM&HC.htm

    The Winery at Holy Cross Abbey   http://www.abbeywinery.com/

Florence   http://www.florencecolorado.net/

Shelf Road, Phantom Canyon Road   http://www.goldbeltbyway.com/

Pueblo   http://www.pueblochamber.org/

    Rocky Mountain Steel Mill   http://www.osm.com/LocationsFacilities/
RockyMountainSteelMills/tabid/71/Default.aspx

    Steelworks Museum of Industry and Culture   http://www.cfisteel.org/

    Rosemount Museum   http://www.rosemount.org/

    El Pueblo Museum   http://www.pueblouniondepot.com/

    Southeast Colorado Heritage Center   http://theheritagecenter.us/

    Pueblo Railway Museum   http://www.pueblorailway.org/

    Pueblo Union Depot   http://www.pueblouniondepot.com/

INDEX

ABOUT THE AUTHOR

LIKE MOST YOUNG BOYS of the 1950s, Claude Wiatrowski enjoyed toy trains. Scale model trains came next, but three degrees—including a doctorate in electrical engineering—and a career in technology slowed his avocation until his first encounter with Colorado's railroads in 1971. Model trains took a backseat to standing on a mountain pass and watching real narrow-gauge steam trains chug past.

Dr. Wiatrowski moved to Colorado in 1975 with his wife, Margaret, and children, Kevin and Karen. Since then, he has authored or provided photographs for several books on Colorado and railroad history, including *Railroads of Colorado* and *Railroads Across North America*. He also produces DVDs about history and railroads. His productions have won Telly and Teddy awards; one was selected for the Library of Congress Local Legacies Program.

Dr. Wiatrowski has played drums for more than fifty years. He currently plays in two big bands and accompanies a gospel quartet, as well as leading his own polka band.

He is a member of the Colorado Midland Chapter of the National Railway Historical Society, the Railway & Locomotive Historical Society, the Colorado Railroad Museum, the Friends of the Cumbres & Toltec Scenic Railroad, the Friends of the East Broad Top, the Nevada Northern Railway Museum, the Pikes Peak Historical Street Railway Foundation, and the Lexington Group in Transportation History.